COLLEGE SUCCESS
FOR **STUDENTS** WITH
PHYSICAL
DISABILITIES

STRATEGIES AND TIPS TO MAKE THE MOST OF YOUR COLLEGE EXPERIENCE

COLLEGE SUCCESS
FOR STUDENTS WITH
PHYSICAL
DISABILITIES

CHRIS WISE TIEDEMANN

PRUFROCK PRESS INC.
WACO, TEXAS

Library of Congress Cataloging-in-Publication Data

Tiedemann, Chris Wise, 1953-
   College success for students with physical disabilities / by Chris Wise Tiedemann.
      p. cm.
   Includes bibliographical references.
   ISBN 978-1-59363-861-0 (pbk.)
   1. College students with disabilities--United States. 2. College student orientation--United States. I. Title.
   LC4231.T54 2012
   371.91--dc23
                        2011045963

Edited by Lacy Compton

Front cover, center image © Wright State University. Used with permission.
Back cover image © University of Houston. Used with permission.

Cover and Layout Design by Raquel Trevino

ISBN-13: 978-1-59363-861-0

At the time of this book's publication, all facts and figures cited are the most current available. All telephone numbers, addresses, and website URLs are accurate and active. All publications, organizations, websites, and other resources exist as described in the book, and all have been verified. The author and Prufrock Press Inc. make no warranty or guarantee concerning the information and materials given out by organizations or content found at websites, and we are not responsible for any changes that occur after this book's publication. If you find an error, please contact Prufrock Press Inc.

Prufrock Press Inc.
P.O. Box 8813
Waco, TX 76714-8813
Phone: (800) 998-2208
Fax: (800) 240-0333
http://www.prufrock.com

DEDICATION

This book is dedicated to the memory of my best college friend, Rick Whitesell, a college success before the law guaranteed him even a high school education; to all students with disabilities who pursue postsecondary education today; and to the wonderful colleges that go out of their way to help those students succeed.

CONTENTS

ACKNOWLEDGEMENTS

Many people made invaluable contributions to the content of this book. First, I wish to thank the four students who agreed to be interviewed about their experiences attending college with a significant physical disability: Kelly Lynn Berger, Dustin Gilmer, Lindsey Newland, and Tommy Tiedemann. May their openness encourage countless others with physical disabilities to pursue their own college dreams.

Thanks also to the disability services directors and professors from disability-friendly colleges across the country who graciously agreed to be interviewed for their insights into college success: Cheryl Amoruso, University of Houston; Jacob Karnes, University of Kentucky; Larry Markle, Ball State University; Jeffrey Vernooy, Wright State University; and Julie Walton, East Stroudsburg University of Pennsylvania. Thanks also to those disability services directors and staffers who contributed suggestions and resources to this project.

I sincerely hope that this effort to illuminate the elements making up a successful college experience for students with physical disabilities will encourage more colleges to offer supports beyond what the law requires.

INTRODUCTION

*Why a Book About College
and Physical Disability?*

FOR the student making the transition from high school, college may represent the first point of passage into the adult world. For those contemplating college following a few years in the workforce or military service, college may be the key to a new occupation or an enhanced quality of life. But whatever their varied and individual reasons for attending college, all students must adjust to a brand-new environment there, according to a 2008 report by the National Council on Disability (NCD).

Yet students with disabilities often enter college unprepared for the new responsibilities and challenges they will face, the report noted. This is because they are often poorly informed about the dramatic differences between their prior educational experiences and the realities of college life—higher academic expectations, greater personal responsibilities, and much different services for people with disabilities, to name a few. Often, too, they have not been prepared to meet the changes they will encounter upon reaching the college campus.

OUR FAMILY'S EXPERIENCE

Our family experienced this firsthand when my son Tommy, who has cerebral palsy, began searching for a college in 2003 and eventually attended three very different types of American colleges. We found information about college success for students with physical disabilities remarkably limited. No books, websites, or college guides. We learned, too, that existing college guidebooks and websites were not written specifically to answer the questions of students with physical disabilities, and even school guidance offices had little information relevant to their special needs. Filling this information gap became an urgent priority for us 2 years before Tommy's high school graduation. Tommy did his senior project in high school on "colleges that accommodate people with disabilities." But even when he was accepted at college and began classes, we often found ourselves working out our own solutions "on the fly" to issues we should have been aware of much earlier.

Eventually we learned the questions to ask, the people to see, and the right way to do things in college (and sometimes, the *wrong* way to do things). So we decided to start a website where families could learn which colleges went beyond the requirements of the law in providing assistance to students with physical disabilities. Our website, http://www.disabilityfriendlycolleges.com, provided a place for students, families, and professionals to read about and discuss these issues. By then, however, we had learned that finding one's best college was only the first mile marker on the road to success in college. A student with physical disabilities must also learn to make use of the college and its disability services and to advocate for his or her own very individual needs.

HOW THIS BOOK CAN HELP YOU

The stories of the students you will read about here prove that students with disabilities *do* experience college success, but they must begin the college search as early as they can, understand how college will be different from high school, learn solid self-determination and self-advocacy skills, and, if possible, plan and prepare for that transition from the early years of high school through the first semester of college.

This book is written for prospective college students, their families, and those who work with them. Its purpose is to provide an introduction to the full range of ingredients in college success, from a student's earliest participation in the IEP process to the time when she regularly and easily discusses her accommodations with her college's disability services office and professors.

Students will learn about their rights under the laws governing education and disability, the meaning and importance of self-advocacy, and perhaps most important, the dramatically different responsibilities and expectations that come along with becoming a college student. They will also learn how having a physical disability affects such college preparation basics as admissions applications, financial aid, and standardized testing. This book will discuss the types of academic and personal accommodations available in college and how to make sure students can get what they need. Finally, each chapter also contains insightful advice from college disability service specialists; resources such as sample forms, planning checklists, and timelines; interviews with college students who have physical disabilities; and profiles of some of the most disability-friendly colleges in the U.S.

Readers who have already completed high school may wish to begin with Chapter 2. Chapters 2–6 cover the college issues mentioned above. Chapter 1 focuses on using the high school years and the IEP process to prepare to go to college with a disability.

ONE SIZE DOES NOT FIT ALL

Students exhibit great variety, and students with physical disabilities are no different. Some students may prefer a college that offers personal services and has hundreds of students with disabilities. Others may prefer to be one of the crowd at their local community college or to pursue an esoteric major at an Ivy League school. All are valid options, and all require that the student understand the college ethic and get ready to meet its requirements for success.

Along the same lines, this book also recognizes that students with physical disabilities can have very different types and combinations of impairments. There is no "one size fits all" recommendation, and students will need to select their college and their services with their own specific needs in mind.

TALKING TO THE EXPERTS

As well as being the mother of a student with a physical disability, I am a professional writer/editor with experience as a journalist, communications manager, and freelance writer. This book approaches postsecondary education and physical disability from the perspective of the student and her family, but it is supported by extensive research with college students and disability service specialists at colleges across the country.

Detailed interviews with four wonderful students appear at the end of each chapter. Kelly Lynn Berger, Dustin Gilmer, Lindsey Newland, and Tommy Tiedemann discuss their experiences with everything from taking the SATs to obtaining personal care services on campus.

Kelly Lynn Berger is a student at the University of Kentucky. She is a journalism major who has congenital muscular dystrophy. Dustin Gilmer, a telecommunications major, attends Ball State University in Indiana. Dustin has polyostotic fibrous dysplasia, also known as Albright syndrome, a brittle bone disorder that also keeps him from growing normally. Lindsey Newland received her bachelor's and master's degrees from the University of Kentucky following her injury in an auto accident. The accident resulted in traumatic brain injury with partial paralysis on the left side of her body. She studied social work with a focus on gerontology. Tommy Tiedemann (my son) is a student at Kennesaw State University in Georgia, where he majors in psychology. As noted, he has cerebral palsy. Tommy has also attended Chattahoochee Technical College and Edinboro University of Pennsylvania. He has therefore experienced three very different types of campus: a technical college, a school known for its extensive services for students with disabilities, and a large state university. These are four smart, frank, and funny young people who never hold back as they bring to life the issues explored in this book.

Lastly, I want to thank my family for the warmth of their affection and support during the year I spent writing this book. No one understands better than Joe and Tommy how important it is that college be made accessible, in as many ways as possible, to those who desire a postsecondary education.

This book was written to help engender in all students the confidence to make good choices and thoroughly enjoy the beauty of the college years. I hope that through reading it, students will recognize that success can come in the form of good grades or a job, but also and more long-lasting, as personal growth, self-knowledge, and an awakened interest in learning.

PLANNING TO SUCCEED IN COLLEGE

By failing to prepare, you are preparing to fail.—Benjamin Franklin

As a student who also has a physical disability, you are already aware of the important role that planning plays in your life. The same is true if you are close to someone who has a physical disability. For example, you know about the importance of parking near curb cuts, giving yourself extra time to get ready for school in the morning, or looking for hotel bathrooms with roll-in showers or grab-bars. Your Individualized Education Program (IEP) at school is, in fact, a plan for your entire K–12 education.

For students going on to college, however, planning does not stop with high school. There are no IEPs in college, but planning becomes even more important because the laws regarding accessibility and accommodation are much different from those that apply to high schools, with the student as chief advocate. Other changes kick in when you advance to college, as well. Perhaps the most important of these is the degree of maturity and responsibility required of successful college students.

In this chapter, you will begin to design a process that will prepare you to find your best college—and to succeed there.

Planning is one of the most important aspects of making a successful transition from high school to college—and the student should always be at the center of that planning process.

COLLEGE IN THE 21ST CENTURY

"My high school was very supportive and expected nothing less of me than to go to college," said Dustin Gilmer, a Ball State University student interviewed for this book. Every one of the students whom you will meet in this book was encouraged to attend college. If you are reading this book, we assume that you, too, are considering college, or that you have made the decision to attend college.

A 2009 U.S. Government Accountability Office study found that 11% of postsecondary students in the U.S. were students with disabilities, and research suggests that this number is growing all of the time. Recent legislation, like the Higher Education Opportunity Act of 2008 and the Post-9/11 Veterans Educational Assistance Act of 2008, contains provisions that assist people with disabilities and may also increase the number of college students with disabilities. So college is indeed a very realistic option.

In terms of college itself, your options include 2-year colleges, 4-year colleges, community and technical colleges, and certificate programs. Your choices are already accumulating.

WHY CHOOSE TO ATTEND COLLEGE

For many people, higher education is fulfilling simply for its own sake and they attend college because they have an intense interest in a particular field or enjoy the academic environment. But for most students, and even for the academically inclined, economics enters the picture as well. People simply need to earn a living.

Students graduating from high school today are entering an economy that is increasingly knowledge based. For example, in 1959, only 20% of workers required some college education for their jobs. Today 56% require college, according to the most recent National Longitudinal Transition Study (NLTS) of students with disabilities (Newman, 2005). You can see that attending college and earning a degree can make a big difference in your future.

EXPECTATIONS VERSUS PREPARATION

Statistics support the idea that young people with disabilities have more college options today and also attend college in larger numbers than ever before. But there are some less heartening statistics, too. The same NLTS study (Newman, 2005) found, for example, that 77% of young people with disabilities in the study had a goal of attending postsecondary school. However, within 2 years of leaving high school, only 31% of youth with disabilities had actually continued on to postsecondary education. The study also noted that similar-aged youth in the general population who do not have disabilities are more than 4 1/2 times as likely to be enrolled in a 4-year college as youth with disabilities. Why is college attendance so much lower for students with disabilities?

Most federal government studies and college disability services directors attribute the lower enrollment to the difference between the expectations of students with disabilities to attend college and the preparation they receive for the reality of college life.

For example, even if well-prepared academically, students in high school are often surprised to learn that there will be no Individualized Education Programs for them in college. In fact, they will not even be asked if they have a disability. If they wish to receive accommodations or assistance from the college's disability services office, they must disclose their disability, provide documentation of it, and request those services themselves. Most colleges are well-prepared to offer the services, but the law requires that the request come from the student.

If you have a physical impairment that interferes with your ability to carry out such functions of daily living as eating, bathing, toileting, or dressing, you may have had a paraprofessional to assist you throughout your public school experience. This is different in college, too. Most colleges require students to provide their own assistance for personal needs, and even assistance in taking notes is usually handled by having a classmate do the note taking.

Unlike K–12 public school, college is not an entitlement. It is one way to continue one's education or preparation for a career, *provided the student has met all of the admissions requirements of the institution.* Once enrolled, the student must continue to meet the college's academic standards and standards of conduct, and the college has the right to dismiss the student if she does not. The college also has the right to maintain the academic integrity of its programs. If this were not the case, a college degree would mean very little. Although colleges are required to make academic and accessibility accommodations, they are not required to make accommodations that would dilute their academic standards.

Moreover, studies show that most college students with disabilities do not choose their institution of higher learning on the basis of its disability services. Like nondisabled students, they choose a college because of its reputation, its location, its curriculum, or its proximity to family or friends. Any prospective college student must be able to assess his needs and preferences carefully when choosing a college.

Given the differences between high school and college and the increased responsibility and maturity required to meet them, it is no wonder that planning is the foundation of college success for students with disabilities. The time to start planning is when you are first considering college as an option—as early as eighth or ninth grade.

YOUR TRANSITION PLAN

Students with physical disabilities can face challenges in public school, but they are fortunate in having a special tool that gives them considerable control over their own education and a planning process to keep it on track. That tool is the IEP process, and it is used in preparing for college as well.

The law governing the K–12 public education of students with disabilities is called the Individuals with Disabilities Education Improvement Act (IDEA). IDEA mandates that each child with a disability should have a written statement containing levels of academic achievement, measurable education goals, accommodations, and other services. This law and those governing college are discussed more fully in Chapter 2, but you are probably already familiar with the fact that the IEP team develops this statement in regularly scheduled meetings throughout your school career.

A part of the IEP process during the later years of public school is called *transition planning*, or preparing for adult life after public school. *Transition services* are those services designed to assist students with disabilities in moving from the world of school to the adult world including college, employment, and other options. IDEA requires transition planning to begin by the time a student is 16. However, if the IEP team decides that transition planning should start earlier, it may do so. For students preparing for college, planning often starts as early as eighth grade. Services should be based on the individual student's needs and should take into account his or her strengths, preferences, and interests (National Dissemination Center for Children with Disabilities [NICHCY], 2010).

WRITE COLLEGE-ORIENTED GOALS

The IEP is an excellent place to begin college planning for two reasons. First, your IEP team can include statements that describe college as your postsecondary goal and then write IEP goals that relate directly to coursework and situations you will encounter in college. Second, you can use the IEP meeting process to develop needed skills in understanding and advocating for your own needs.

IEP goals must be concrete and measurable. Your IEP team probably includes you, your parents, teachers, school administrators, and others as needed. The professional educators on the team can help craft language that leads to measurable goals. However, you and your family should be sure to include goals such as the following:

- ▶ completing specific coursework for a college preparatory diploma,
- ▶ obtaining an evaluation for the use of assistive technology,
- ▶ practicing self-advocacy skills, and
- ▶ practicing instructing those who assist you with personal care activities.

DISABILITY SERVICES TIP

College disability services directors stress that the written IEP statement should carefully list those skills that the student will need for college and include goals to ensure that the student works on those skills while still in high school.

SELF-ADVOCACY SKILLS

Building self-advocacy skills is one of the most important goals for students with disabilities while still in high school. This means being able to describe one's own disability and request appropriate accommodations. One of the best ways to build these skills, disability services specialists say, is for you to gradually increase your participation in your IEP meetings, perhaps with the goal of eventually leading the meeting.

In your early years in public school, your parents or guardians represented you at IEP meetings. Parents of students with disabilities learn to advocate effectively at these sessions, sometimes obtaining assistance or coaching from outside organizations such as state advocacy offices or the organization Parent to Parent. However, you, the student, must be invited to any IEP meeting where postsecondary goals and transition services will be considered. Building on research that shows the importance of self-determination and self-advocacy for the college success of students with disabilities, emphasis has been placed in recent years not only on including the student in the IEP meetings, but also on gradually increasing his role.

An article in *Teaching Exceptional Children* (Mason, McGahee-Kovac, & Johnson, 2004) cited three levels of involvement in the IEP meeting that gradually increase the student's role:

- ▶ **Level 1**—Student presents information about or reads from his or her transition plan for the future.
- ▶ **Level 2**—Student explains his or her disability, shares information on individual strengths and weaknesses (present levels of performance), and explains the accommodations needed. Students present Level 1 information and may suggest new IEP goals.
- ▶ **Level 3**—Student leads the IEP conference, including Level 1 and Level 2 responsibilities, introductions, and closing.

DISABILITY SERVICES TIP

Self-advocacy is something students with physical disabilities should be spending more time learning in high school today, disability services directors say. Some students come to college unaware of the importance of self-advocacy, others have difficulty doing it, and still others have always had it done for them, noted Jacob Karnes, director of the Disability Resource Center at the University of Kentucky. Students who work on self-advocacy in high school have a head start on the maturity and responsibility necessary for college success

One final note to students: Even if you believe you are ready to move on to college, remember that students with disabilities who are served under an IEP may stay in the public education system until age 21. High school coursework and the college search are both very time-consuming. You may want to take advantage of this option and plan to spend one more year in high school if you need more time to research and visit colleges or perhaps improve your grades or your scores on standardized tests before beginning college.

THE PARENT'S ROLE

On my website, http://www.disabilityfriendlycolleges.com, many of the questions I receive about preparing for and finding colleges come from parents and even grandparents. Just as successfully adapting to college life requires responsibility and maturity, adjusting to life as the parent of a college student requires flexibility and an open mind. In some ways, the parent may need even more perseverance than the student, but perseverance has its reward in the emergence of a capable, successful college student.

LETTING GO

As one college disability services director noted, "This is a child that you have cared for since birth, or since a disabling injury occurred, so it is not easy to start to let go and allow the child to take over." If the child is one who does not relish the self-advocacy role, it can be even tougher.

Unfortunately, as some colleges stress, students cannot be prepared to manage their disabilities if they have never done so. For example, a student will be much better prepared to succeed if she has learned to handle her personal care, shopping, medical, and equipment issues herself rather than having them all handled by her parents up until she begins college.

Parental "overadvocacy" occurs in the academic realm, as well. On college visits and admissions interviews, do not answer for your child or tell administrators what accommodations she will need. This is the time for your student to begin speaking up and saying, "These are some of the accommodations I have in high school . . ." Practicing and role-playing before visiting an admissions counselor or disability services officer is a great idea. However, it is more important to give your student experience advocating for her needs and explaining her disability than it is to get everything exactly right. As the administrators meet your child for the first time, it is important that they see that she can convey her own interests and needs and that she understands them herself.

STAYING CLOSE

The fact that parents must start to "back off" as their student takes on the challenge of preparing for college does not mean they should not provide guidance and, especially, encouragement. You are the best judge of your child's level of maturity and readiness for this new role. Just as with parents of nondisabled students, "a parent's mentoring relationship must be based on an underlying trust and respect for one's child as someone capable of learning how to manage his or her own life" (National Center on Secondary Education and Transition [NCSET], 2004, para. 3).

See the Resources section of this chapter for a College Planning Timeline for Parents designed to help you keep your student on track for college success.

COLLEGE PLANNING TIMELINE FOR STUDENTS

Serious college planning usually begins early in high school. Many students have not given much thought to postsecondary education before that time. Some experts even say that placing too much emphasis on getting into college too early can do more harm than good to a student. However, a little bit of early planning, especially as it relates to the IEP process, is useful for students with disabilities as early as middle school.

Middle School

Middle school grades will not appear on the transcripts you send to colleges, but by this time you should be attending at least a portion of your IEP meeting and listening to teachers explain high school course requirements. If you are certain about going to college, then take a look at websites and college catalogs to see the admissions requirements and prepare your upcoming high school schedule accordingly. If you are undecided, keep all options open by planning on a college prep schedule. Make sure your IEP includes a transition plan, even if it is not required until age 16.

Ninth Grade

Discussing college and career options with your guidance counselor or academic advisor should be a high priority this first year of high school. If your school has not assigned you a counselor or scheduled this meeting, request it yourself. Try out some high school extracurricular activities or join community organizations or church groups; colleges like to see participation. As with every year in school, read,

read, read. And remember, grades from here on go on the high school transcript, so work hard.

For students with physical disabilities, it is important to prepare a little bit each year to take over responsibility for your own affairs in college. This year, practice doing your own personal shopping and using and budgeting money. If you need help organizing and planning your schoolwork, include study skills classes in your schedule.

More tips for freshman year:

- ▶ Take college prep courses. If you need a foreign language and speech is an issue, try Latin; it is not a spoken language and thus requires little conversation.
- ▶ If you live or travel near a college, visit its campus.
- ▶ Begin doing research (utilize the Internet, books, and your personal physicians) to help you understand your disability.
- ▶ Include working with different types of assistive technology in your IEP.
- ▶ Attend your IEP meetings. If you feel overwhelmed or uncomfortable, ask for help from teachers or parents to prepare to participate.
- ▶ Set up a long-range plan with your counselor or orthopedically impaired (OI) teacher for taking college entrance exams and applying for the appropriate accommodations.

Tenth Grade

Continue to meet with your guidance counselor to discuss your postsecondary education goals. Consider asking about career interest assessments. Keep up your grades, read from high school reading lists and beyond, and participate in extracurricular and community activities.

You now have a year of high school under your belt, so it's time to look at the differences you will encounter in college. The next chapter will cover this in depth. The disability services pages of college websites are another great place to find information on this topic.

More sophomore year tips:

- ▶ Take the PSAT as practice for the SAT; discuss your results with your advisor.
- ▶ Continue to look into college requirements, and make sure your high school courses match them.

▶ If writing does not come easily to you, ask for coaching from a supportive English teacher.

▶ Begin to think about the college environment that suits you. Consider college size, location, city or rural, and so forth.

▶ Continue to learn money management skills from your family and organizational skills at school. Begin to selectively use a credit card—with parental controls.

▶ Attend your IEP meetings. Give your input during discussions. If you would like to take a more active leadership role, request some training and practice to do so.

ELEVENTH GRADE

Junior year is where the action is in college preparation: college entrance exams, the last full year of grades that will go with your college applications, and some serious sleuthing to find the absolute best fit in colleges. If you are taking the SAT or ACT, have your advisor apply for appropriate accommodations for you in plenty of time. Listen to college recruiters at your school, or attend college fairs. Collect pertinent information about the colleges you are considering such as course offerings, location, tuition and fees, admission requirements, and class size. Continue to read and participate in extracurriculars or volunteering. A summer job or internship will look great on your college application.

Personal care will be your own responsibility when living on campus at most schools. Look into independent living training, perhaps over the summer, or begin working on such issues as hiring and directing personal care, managing money, and dealing with health issues. Ramp up your participation in the IEP and make sure all services are in place for you to make the most of the college you choose.

More tips for eleventh grade:

▶ Continue meeting with your counselor and IEP team to review the courses you've completed, courses still needed, and any remedial work needed.

▶ Be aware of your class rank when applying to colleges. Your counselor can tell you this.

▶ Begin using the information you've gathered to narrow down your college list to the five or six that interest you most. Share your thoughts on the colleges' strengths and weaknesses with your family.

- Begin making college visits at schools near home or those you pass during vacation.
- Make contact with the state Vocational Rehabilitation (VR) department and see what services they can offer you to assist with college. They can help you apply for social security benefits and Medicaid. Obtain a social security number if you don't already have one.
- If you plan to apply for financial aid, be sure to attend information programs at your high school and request information from colleges that interest you.
- Summer is a good time to review the disability services websites of colleges you are interested in to see what type of documentation of disabilities you will need to provide.
- Organize a filing system for all of the college information and paperwork you will acquire during senior year.
- Review and keep a calendar of college application deadlines.

Twelfth Grade

In senior year, most activities related to college are specific to either the fall or spring semester, and some things must be done after graduation. As with the other 3 years of high school, it's important to keep up your grades and make sure that you have the correct courses and credits to graduate in the spring. Continued participation in extracurricular activities and the community will look positive on your college applications.

Fall semester tips:

- Cut back on academic modifications that either will not be available in college or you no longer need.
- Continue your research on scholarships and grants, consulting with your guidance counselor and the colleges you visit.
- Send in your college application forms and fees and any financial aid forms required now. Keep copies.
- Take the ACT and/or SAT, if required by your colleges. Allow plenty of time for your advisor to apply for accommodations. Have your scores sent to the colleges to which you plan to apply.

Spring semester tips:

► Fill out and submit the Free Application for Federal Student Aid (FAFSA; http://www.fafsa.ed.gov) after January 1. Forms are also available at guidance offices.

► Make any final campus visits.

► Make your college selection and notify the schools to which you were accepted. Send the deposit to the school of your choice; have your guidance counselor send your final transcript to this college. Complete the paperwork the college sends to you.

► Prepare any documentation required by disability services at the college of your choice, including any from medical professionals.

► If you have not already, have an assistive technology evaluation to see what hardware and software might help with college work and match what's available at the college you've selected. Obtain training on these.

CONCLUSION

College is a very realistic option for students with physical disabilities, and it has been so for some time. However, there will be many differences between attending college and being a high school student. Many things that have been provided for you or done for you in high school will be different in college. That is why it is so important to begin planning early for your college education and to include your plans formally in your IEP. Utilizing the timelines in this chapter, you can stay on top of your college preparation each year and include the appropriate courses, activities, and training in your IEP.

Your next step will be to begin your own investigation of your college options. In order to evaluate the colleges you locate, you will need a firm understanding of the differences between high school and college as well as of the laws governing your education as a student with a disability.

STUDENT INTERVIEWS

In what year of school did you really begin thinking about and planning for college?

Kelly: Well, I have an older sister, and she started looking at colleges before me, so I decided to go along with her because I knew in a couple of years that I would be looking myself. So, I would say my freshman year in high school. I started early and was prepared. But I had my dream college set in mind to begin with.

Lindsey: Junior year (pre-disability).

Tommy: I think in my junior year of high school, I began to think about college and where I wanted to go.

Describe the steps you took to help begin the transition process for college. Explain anything you wish you had done better to prepare.

Kelly: To transition, I toured the campus with the rest of the campus tour group and then made several visits alone with my mom where we personally went around campus ourselves and pointed out different issues that needed to be addressed before I got there. In a big group it's really hard to follow along and figure out the accessible ways. So, going around and exploring separately helped me gain my confidence and become more familiar with the most accessible pathways.

Tommy: I talked to my OI (orthopedically impaired) teacher first. She asked me a lot of questions about whether I wanted to go away to school or stay home. Then she asked me more questions because she was trying to get a sense of what I really wanted to do. We met with my VR counselor and talked about the same sorts of things. I had some idea what I wanted to do and she asked me about what courses of study I wanted to pursue. I didn't know at that time yet that I wanted to go away to college, but that idea began to grow on me. I began visiting colleges when a friend who also has CP went away to college.

Then there was my senior project. It was a project we were required to complete in senior year and it included a research paper, work with a mentor, and a presentation. I did mine on "Colleges That Accommodate People With Physical Disabilities." Doing this research I found Edinboro and Wright State universities and a couple other colleges.

Dustin: I started by looking for places of my own interest and didn't really worry about the things that needed to be done due to my disability. It just so happened that Ball State University was one of the top schools in both telecommunications and accessibility for disabled students.

What were your best resources in both college planning and finding the schools that had the best education and services for you?

Kelly: Well, basically just visiting the colleges you are interested in and seeing if it is physically possible to attend there, talking with the tour guides, and then reaching out to the Disability Resource Center on campus to see how others have gotten around in my situation.

Lindsey: My VR counselor and my high school counselors.

Tommy: Some were from my high school. My OI teacher helped me with research materials from the guidance office. She acted as my counselor, and I never saw anyone from the guidance office. But I found most of my information doing research with my mentor for my senior project. He is the director of the Disabilities Ministry for the Catholic Archdiocese of Atlanta. He knew a lot of organizations and people to contact and we did.

Dustin: When I originally started looking I found that everyone told me, "Oh, there are great schools out there and you should have no problem finding funding for school because there are plenty of grants and scholarships for disabled students." However, no one could seem to tell me where to look. I had to basically discover it for myself. I used the Internet mostly.

How supportive was your high school of your college ambitions?

Kelly: Yes, they definitely pushed me and made me feel that there really wasn't any other option. They thought it was a great opportunity and that I would do great things here and help "change the system" in a way to adapt it to make it work for me.

Tommy: I'd say that [my school] was really supportive of my wanting to go to college. They did assume that I would go to college.

How useful was the IEP in preparing you for college? What was the degree of your participation in it?

Kelly: They were very useful to give my teachers, staff, and principals an insight into my daily needs and activities that I would need adapted. I'm definitely a private person and don't like my needs to be addressed in front of the whole class, so noting this and explaining this during the meeting was key for me. It was hard for me to even explain to them what I go through on a daily basis and how they can help; it is sometimes embarrassing but definitely necessary and effective.

Tommy: The IEP was very useful for me because it listed what I had to do in terms of courses to prepare for college. At first, I didn't participate, but then later on I became quite involved.

Dustin: I hated my IEP meetings. I felt like they were pointless, especially because they took time out of my classes. I was always in regular classes, nothing special and never really needed any extra assistance because I strive to be as independent as possible. That meant whatever it took for me to do the things the other students did I would figure out ways to do that myself.

What things did you do during high school to learn to advocate for your interests and needs?

Kelly: I would say learning from experience. I was definitely the shyest person ever in high school and absolutely hated to ask for help. So any time I had to ask for someone to open the door for me, I would get all nervous and red in the face. Everyone always told me, "Speak up, Kelly, just ask, you need to be louder!" It took it a while for me to catch on, and I would still be that same person if I had not gone away to college by myself and learned to speak up and stand my ground. Something about being on your own and struggling makes asking strangers for help a lot easier.

Tommy: My OI teacher helped by encouraging me to speak up, but eventually I just decided to do it. I just got tired of people talking about and for me.

CHAPTER 1 RESOURCES

COLLEGE PLANNING TIMELINE FOR PARENTS

Independence, self-determination, and self-advocacy are essential for students with disabilities. That does not mean parents should take their eyes off the ball, however. Here are a few areas for parents to keep an unobtrusive eye on.

Ninth Grade

- Begin teaching your student to handle money and credit cards.
- Begin discussing career and college options with your student.
- Stay involved with the IEP process, but encourage a larger role for your student.
- Begin researching colleges with an eye toward those that are disability friendly.
- Encourage self-advocacy in your child and be sure his school does, too.
- Keep your student registered for a college-prep track in high school and working toward a college-prep diploma.
- Read your child's school website or newsletter for college planning information.

Tenth Grade

- More strongly encourage your child to participate in the IEP meeting and see that she receives training if necessary at school.
- Encourage your student to do his own college phone and Internet research, but be available to help, especially if it is physically difficult.
- Get your student more involved in her own medical care issues, including speaking to physicians herself on office visits.
- Research the financial side of college to determine realistic school choices and scholarships and aid available.

Eleventh Grade

- In many ways this is the most important year in the college search. Make sure your student stays on top of schoolwork *and* continues to research and visit colleges.

- ▶ Thoroughly understand the differences between high school and college. They are many, so check out Chapter 2.
- ▶ *Do not* speak for your child on college visits; *do* help her prepare in advance.
- ▶ Find out what disability services departments will require as documentation for your child's disability and make sure your family has this documentation.
- ▶ Stay on top of college entrance exam and college application deadlines this year and next. Students with disabilities must apply early for entrance exam accommodations.
- ▶ If your student plans to live on a campus where personal care assistance is not provided, this is the time to get some experience with independent living training or at least directing others besides family to do her care.

Twelfth Grade

- ▶ The home stretch! Stay on top of grades, deadlines, and calming your student's nerves.
- ▶ Make sure your student is working with a Vocational Rehabilitation counselor.
- ▶ Students should be speaking for themselves at IEPs and leading the meeting, if possible.
- ▶ Give your student any help she needs in completing and reviewing applications.
- ▶ Be sure your student has a technology evaluation for college technology and computer aids.
- ▶ Parents have deadlines, too, especially for financial aid. Complete your FAFSA after you file your taxes this year! Compare financial aid offers your student receives.
- ▶ Make sure your student stays on top of application status, either online or by phone.
- ▶ Help and support your student through the final decision.
- ▶ Assist your student over the summer to stay in close contact with disability services and put all necessary supports in place for the fall semester.
- ▶ Stay in close personal touch during the freshman year of college—don't take anything for granted!

WEBSITES RELATED TO CHAPTER 1

Association on Higher Education and Disability (AHEAD)

http://www.ahead.org

AHEAD is a professional organization for individuals involved in the development of policy and in the provision of services to persons with disabilities involved in all areas of higher education.

Check out the Students and Parents section for transition and college resources.

HEATH Resource Center

http://www.heath.gwu.edu

The HEATH Resource Center is an online clearinghouse on postsecondary education for individuals with disabilities. The HEATH website has many detailed materials on transition, parenting, and college.

National Center on Secondary Education and Transition (NCSET)

http://www.ncset.org

NCSET coordinates national resources, offers technical assistance, and disseminates information related to secondary education and transition for youth with disabilities. The sections on transition planning, postsecondary education, and parenting postsecondary students are excellent.

National Dissemination Center for Children with Disabilities (NICHCY)

http://www.nichcy.org

NICHCY is a central source of information on children and disabilities, research-based educational practices, and IDEA. The sections on publications and transition to adulthood are especially helpful.

National Secondary Transition Technical Assistance Center (NSTTAC)

http://www.nsttac.org

This website helps educators to prepare students for transition including participating in IEP meetings to the greatest extent possible.

Striving & Thriving: A Guide for College-Bound Students With Disabilities

http://www.wright.edu/students/dis_services/dvd.html

This video describes not only the many experiences of physically disabled students at Wright State University, but also the realities of college life and the transition to college. It features actual Wright State students.

[WHAT YOU CAN EXPECT FROM COLLEGE]

STUDENTS moving from high school to college find that along with the "upgrade" from high school student to college undergraduate, there are also increased academic demands and responsibilities.

For students with physical disabilities, there are also significant changes in the rules about academic and personal accommodations. Soon you will begin to sift through college websites and literature and make college visits. To do so you must know what to expect from colleges, understand the accommodations to which you are entitled, and have the skills necessary to obtain the accommodations you need.

THE LAW AND COLLEGES

In the United States, the three primary laws that govern the education of people who have physical disabilities are the Individuals with Disabilities Education Improvement Act (IDEA), Section 504 of the Rehabilitation Act of 1973, and Title II of the Americans with Disabilities Act of 1990. IDEA guarantees that every child with a disability has a right to receive a free appropriate public education. Section 504 of the Rehabilitation Act of 1973 and Title II of the Americans with Disabilities Act of 1990 protect postsecondary students with disabilities from discrimination.

IDEA

Before Congress passed the Education for All Handicapped Children Act of 1975, the educational needs of millions of American children with disabilities were not being met. Often these students were excluded entirely from the public school system. This act, later renamed the Individuals with Disabilities Education Improvement Act (IDEA, 2004), ensures that children with disabilities have access to a free appropriate public education.

IDEA requires that this education emphasize the special education needs and services of children with disabilities and provide them with an Individualized Education Program (IEP) that meets IDEA's requirements. The content, methodology, or delivery of instruction is adapted to ensure the child's access to the curriculum (National Dissemination Center for Children With Disabilities [NICHCY], 2009). The most recent amendments to IDEA were passed by Congress in 2004, and final regulations were published in 2006. IDEA applies only to students in grades K–12.

SECTION 504 OF THE REHABILITATION ACT OF 1973

This law prohibits discrimination on the basis of disability by any program or activity receiving federal financial assistance. Virtually all public and most private colleges do receive federal financial assistance. If you are interested in a private college, be sure to find out if it receives federal funding and is therefore covered by Section 504.

A person with a disability is defined by Section 504 as any person who "has a physical or mental impairment which substantially limits one or more of such person's major life activities; has a record of such impairment or is regarded as having such impairment" (Association on Higher Education and Disability [AHEAD], n.d., p. 1). Section 504 protects the civil rights of persons who are academically and technically qualified to participate in a program but are disabled.

Under Section 504, students with documented disabilities may request modifications, accommodations, or aids that help them to participate in all postsecondary education programs and activities.

It is very important to understand that the student must request any accommodations and modifications and that the college or university has the flexibility to select the specific aid or service it provides, as long as it is effective. Examples of modifications that a school might provide include removal of architectural barriers, provision of note takers, extra time on exams, and changing test formats. Colleges may, but need not, provide personal aids such as personal assistants and wheelchairs.

Section 504 does not require that every aspect of every facility be made accessible. Rather, it says that the program should be accessible when viewed in its entirety. This may mean relocating a class or providing a service in an accessible location. New construction on a campus, however, is subject to Section 504 (Rothstein, 1993).

AMERICANS WITH DISABILITIES ACT

The Americans with Disabilities Act (ADA) of 1990 is the civil rights guarantee for persons with disabilities in the United States. It provides protection from discrimination for individuals on the basis of disability. It extends the civil rights protections for people with disabilities to employment in the public and private sectors, transportation, public accommodations, services provided by state and local government, nonprofit service providers, and telecommunications services.

ADA upholds and extends the standards for compliance set forth in Section 504, discussed above, to policies and procedures that impact the treatment of students with disabilities (AHEAD, 2001).

ADA essentially provides no more protection than Section 504. Under Section 504, programs receiving federal financial assistance are already prohibited from discriminating on the basis of disability. Colleges must not discriminate on the basis of disability, but students must be qualified to fulfill the requirements of the program. Institutions are not required to provide accommodations that would be "unduly burdensome" either in an administrative or a financial sense (Rothstein, 1993).

According to the Office for Civil Rights of the U.S. Department of Education (2005), a college is not required to provide the free and appropriate education mandated for high schools in IDEA, but rather "appropriate academic adjustments as necessary to ensure it does not discriminate" (p. 1).

FAMILY EDUCATION RIGHTS AND PRIVACY ACT (FERPA)

FERPA transfers any rights formerly given to parents over to the student at age 18 or upon entering college. This means that college records, whether academic or disability-related, cannot be disclosed to others, including parents, without the permission of the student.

HOW COLLEGE DIFFERS FROM HIGH SCHOOL

College students are responsible for obtaining their own accommodations under these laws, but college differs from high school in many other ways as well.

Tables 1–3 summarize how academics, student responsibilities, and personal services are governed in both types of institutions so that students may anticipate and prepare for these differences.

ADVOCATING FOR ACCOMMODATIONS

Although college brings changes, there will be many services and accommodations available there for students with disabilities. Most colleges list them on their websites on the disability services page. As you consider what services you will need, carefully review the modifications you receive in high school (e.g., extra time on tests, scribes) and consider which ones might no longer be necessary before committing to them in college.

DISABILITY SERVICES TIP

Strive for academic independence. "There are needs you will have for assistance, but the more you place responsibility on others, the more they can mess up your schedule," said Jeffrey A. Vernooy, director, Office of Disability Services, Wright State University.

MOBILITY IMPAIRMENTS

Students may have a variety of different physical disabilities. Some students may have conditions they were born with, while others may have become disabled through accidents, illness, or military service. Students with the following conditions may need to request accommodations through the college disability services office:

▶ **Amputation.** Removal of one or more limbs; for example, by trauma or by surgery.

Table 1

Academic Differences Between High School and College

High School	College
Students spend about 6 hours a day in school, 5 days a week. The school year lasts about 9 months.	Students spend about 12–16 hours a week in class. A year is either two semesters or four quarters.
Students may spend anywhere from no time to 2–3 hours outside of class studying.	For each hour spent in class, students study roughly 2–3 hours outside of class.
Students read short assignments. These are discussed in class and often are retaught.	Expect a large amount of reading. It may or may not be discussed in class. Professors will assume that students have read the material, and they will be expected to know it on tests.
Tests and quizzes are given often and cover relatively small amounts of material.	Tests may be given only once or twice a semester and may cover weeks of material.
Teachers give much feedback and check to see if students are having difficulty with material.	Professors are available for help, but students must request it as well as feedback.
Students with physical disabilities are assigned a paraprofessional to write notes, assignments, and tests.	Disability services office assists students with note-taking and test-taking arrangements. Student must request these services in advance.

- ▶ **Arthritis.** Inflammation of the joints, causing pain and difficult movement.
- ▶ **Cerebral palsy.** A condition resulting from damage to the brain, usually during fetal development or the birth process. Cerebral palsy affects body movement and coordination of the muscles and can cause delay in motor development and spasticity. Students may have difficulty with mobility, writing, or speech.
- ▶ **Muscular dystrophies.** A group of hereditary degenerative disorders that cause progressive muscular atrophy and weakness.
- ▶ **Multiple sclerosis.** A chronic disease that attacks the central nervous system, multiple sclerosis is often disabling. MS can develop at any age, but is most likely to occur between the ages of 20 and 40. Symptoms can range from mild (numbness

Table 2

Differences in Student Responsibility Between High School and College

High School	College
Students have a set schedule and are supervised while at school.	Students make their own schedules and have more unscheduled time.
Attendance is taken every day.	Attendance is not required. Students learn from experience that missing class leads to poor knowledge of the material and low grades.
Counselors advise students, who then fill out and submit course schedules.	Students must choose their own courses, avoid course conflicts, and stay on top of graduation requirements and prerequisites. Academic advisors are available to help.
Teachers make sure students receive material missed due to absence.	Students must find out what they have missed due to absence. Getting contact information for at least one classmate is a good idea if lecture notes are not posted online.
School staff arranges support services for students with disabilities.	Students become clients of the disability services office and arrange all accommodations and support through them.
Parent permission is required until 18 years of age.	Student is considered an adult and is responsible for all decision making. Parent permission is no longer required.

of the limbs) to severe (paralysis). Progress and specific symptoms of the disease vary from one person to another and are unpredictable.

► **Paraplegia.** Paralysis of the legs and lower part of the body. Paraplegia often involves loss of sensation as well as loss of motion. It is the result of damage to the spinal cord.

► **Quadriplegia.** Paralysis of both arms and both legs. Respiration may also be affected if the upper cervical region of the spinal cord is damaged.

► **Spina bifida.** A neural tube defect in which the spinal column does not close up all the way while a child is in the womb. Dis-

Table 3

Differences Between Disability Services in High School and College

High School	College
Students and parents are part of a team that determines placement, service, and supports within school and writes them into the IEP.	There is no IEP process or modifications to the program. Students identify themselves as needing accommodations and provide documentation to obtain them.
The plan made by the IEP team is known by all involved school personnel.	The student makes contact with disability services and with professors. No one is contacted without the student's permission.
Personal care services and therapies are provided by the school system.	Colleges are not required to provide personal care services. A very small number do provide them; some others help students to obtain them.
Teachers are expected to learn as much as possible about the disabilities of their students.	Professors are required to learn only what is related to the accommodations the student receives.

ability can be moderate or severe depending on the form of spina bifida present.

▶ **Traumatic brain injury.** Caused by a bump, blow, or jolt to the head or by a penetrating head injury, TBI disrupts the normal function of the brain. TBI may be mild (change in consciousness) or more severe (extended unconsciousness or amnesia).

A physical disability is often unaccompanied by cognitive or other disabilities. However, in some conditions, such as cerebral palsy, the mobility impairment may be accompanied by cognitive disabilities or difficulty in hearing, seeing, or speaking.

Accommodations. With these definitions in mind, what are some of the most frequently requested accommodations for college students with physical disabilities? Accommodations may include:

▶ accessible classroom furniture,
▶ accessible transportation,

- adapted physical education/sports,
- assistive technology,
- attendant care (only a few colleges offer this but many will help you find it),
- disabled parking,
- elevators and lifts,
- exam accommodations,
- housing accommodations,
- loaner wheelchairs,
- note takers,
- preferential seating,
- priority registration,
- reduced course load,
- relocation of classrooms to accessible locations,
- shuttle transportation,
- snow removal, and
- wheelchair repair.

DISABILITY SERVICES TIP

Disability services directors are unanimous in saying that the biggest hurdle for students with physical disabilities is learning to obtain and direct personal care services at college. In the words of one director, "Understand personal care and what you can do and what kinds of assistance you need. There won't be any academics if you can't get out of bed."

CHRONIC DISEASES AND MEDICAL CONDITIONS

Medical conditions and chronic illnesses are another category of disabilities that may require accommodations in the postsecondary setting. These are health-related conditions that result in a person being considered disabled under the ADA definition because of an impairment that substantially limits one's ability to engage in one or more life activities. If a chronic disease substantially impacts an individual's ability to perform activities of this kind, then it may be classified by college disability service providers as a disability.

Typically, a student with a chronic disease or a medical condition who is requesting accommodations must submit documentation from a medical professional about the nature and extent of her condition. Disability professionals at the college will then determine whether or not the symptoms or effects of treatment raise the condition to the level of being a disability.

Examples of chronic diseases and medical conditions that might require postsecondary accommodations include, but are not limited to, diabetes, cancer, autoimmune disorders, respiratory conditions, seizure disorders, cardiac disorders, AIDS, and pain syndromes.

Sometimes, too, the side effects of medications or the combinations of symptoms impact the individual's ability to perform major life activities. Some symptoms of medical and chronic disabilities in college students might be difficulty walking, sitting, or standing for long periods; difficulty carrying books or computers; unpredictable energy levels; chronic pain; and difficulty with concentration.

Accommodations. Because of the wide variety of possible medical conditions and chronic diseases and their treatment effects, there are a number of accommodations requested by students. These may include (AHEAD, 2002):

- ► priority scheduling,
- ► reduced course load,
- ► parking close to classes,
- ► note takers,
- ► extended time,
- ► early access to the course syllabus or assignments, and
- ► special seating and assistive technology.

SELF-ADVOCACY AND SELF-DETERMINATION

Colleges offer a variety of accommodations to students with disabilities. But once a student has graduated from high school and entered college, she is responsible for advocating for her own accommodations and services.

Chapter 1 discussed the importance of gaining self-advocacy experience through the IEP process. It is helpful to review the concepts of self-advocacy and self-determination here as well, because they are essential to both assessing the accommodations you will need and obtaining them.

Self-advocacy and self-determination are so closely connected that sometimes they are used interchangeably. *Self-advocacy* for college students, however, means taking up one's own cause, or actively seeking the help you need to pursue your goals while in college. Some students develop excellent self-advocacy skills in high school. Others, perhaps because of a speech impediment or reliance on strong parental advocates, may need to practice this skill. That is why self-advocacy experience should be included in the IEP.

Self-determination is described by Field, Martin, Miller, Ward, and Wehmeyer as "a combination of skills, knowledge, and beliefs that enable a person to engage in goal-directed, self-regulated, autonomous behavior" (as cited in Wehmeyer, 2002, para. 3). They stressed the importance of understanding one's own strengths and limitations and the belief in oneself as a capable person. Wehmeyer's (2002) article also described self-determined people as "knowing what they want and how to get it" and as "people who make things happen in their lives" (para. 4–5).

Students who can successfully manage their coursework and accommodations must have both self-advocacy skills and self-determination in their toolkit.

ENABLING COLLEGES

The academic and personal environment at most American colleges will be quite different from what the student with a physical disability experienced in high school. However, there are a handful of colleges that endeavor to combine a supportive environment with academic rigor and training to live independently. Students who need substantial personal care support or who feel more comfortable in a setting where disabilities are common among fellow students may wish to consider this type of college. Further information on these colleges can be found in the Resources sections at the end of this and subsequent chapters. Each school has its own philosophy regarding personal independence and how best to get there. The prospective student must determine if one of these philosophies fits her unique needs. You will also find at the end of this book a listing of "America's Most Disability-Friendly Colleges," colleges that either offer this high level of support or go beyond the requirements of the ADA in offering accommodations.

OTHER DISABILITY-FRIENDLY OPTIONS

Although they do not go as far as the five I feature in this book in providing disability services, a number of colleges and universities across America do go beyond the letter of the ADA. Always be sure to talk to disability services representatives at any college in which you are interested. For more information on specific colleges, see our website, http://www.disabilityfriendlycolleges.com, or the list of America's most disability-friendly colleges at the end of this book.

UNIVERSAL DESIGN AND ACCESSIBILITY

A number of universities are adopting the principles of universal design when constructing new facilities on campus, scheduling courses, and designing websites. Universal design is "the design of products and environments to be usable by all people, to the greatest extent possible, without the need for adaptation or specialized design" (North Carolina State University, 1997, para. 1).

A relatively new way to consider blending the needs of those with disabilities, those without disabilities, and those with other special needs, universal design is used in postsecondary education to render the academic environment and curriculum accessible to all students. By viewing disabilities as natural differences among students, universal design encourages the university community as a whole to plan the educational experience to meet the needs of all learners.

For example, universities may address the needs of students with disabilities or illnesses in accessing the curriculum by providing flexible scheduling and course websites that contain a complete syllabus, daily class notes, and even streaming video of lectures (AHEAD, 2002).

With regard to physical accessibility, universal design means incorporating simple features such as room for wheelchairs to turn in any direction, hallways with room for two wheelchairs to pass, lever door handles, and lecture halls with accessible seating scattered throughout the room to promote choice for students.

Universal design works best in situations involving new construction. The University of Wisconsin-Whitewater and the University at Buffalo (part of the State University of New York system) are two schools that have received recognition for accommodating both disabled and nondisabled students this way.

However, universal design does not replace the ADA requirements all schools must meet or the need for accommodations when it does not adequately improve access for someone. It does help a campus demonstrate a positive attitude toward persons with disabilities and work to foster a welcoming and inclusive atmosphere.

CONCLUSION

College has a much different atmosphere from high school. There is more freedom, more responsibility is demanded of students, and fewer services and accommodations are available for most students with disabilities. College is, after all, the last place in the transition to becoming a working adult where there will actually be an office that offers accommodations and services. It is where a student learns to navigate independently in the world.

Beginning the college search without a sound understanding of the changes and the laws involved sets a student back months or even years. Having acquired that information, readers of this book are now ready to take the plunge into the college selection and application process.

To help in that process, each chapter's Resources section from here on contains a thumbnail sketch of one of America's most disability-friendly colleges. These colleges offer the most significant number of services and accommodations sought by students with physical disabilities.

STUDENT INTERVIEWS

What differences between college and high school were you aware of before you got to college?

Kelly: I definitely knew coming into college that I was getting into a lot. The workload was huge. I had an older sister who filled me in on this and gave me some advice on what to expect, so I thought I had a clue.

Tommy: I was aware of a lot of differences even though I had not experienced them yet. I learned about the laws and the different responsibilities students have in college through my research project in high school. Knowing about the differences in workload and responsibility is not the same as experiencing them, though. I think what I came face-to-face with when I was finally living 800 miles from home was the amount of maturity it was going to require to be able to manage my academics and my own personal and social issues for the first time with no one looking over my shoulder—things like keeping up with work, getting to class on time, knowing when to go to a doctor if I didn't feel well, and staying in touch with my family.

Dustin: I realized that college classes would be much more difficult and would require more studying than in high school. I realized that ultimately I'm responsible for anything I do. No more parents taking the consequences; it's all on me.

What did you know about the responsibilities of students once they enter college, as compared to high school?

Kelly: I knew that you're basically on your own the whole way. In college they don't make you do anything; it's all on you. You have to be motivated and have that drive to succeed if you really want to make it through all of your classes and get good grades.

Tommy: I knew that it is up to you to do the work and to turn it in. The responsibility falls more on you, the student. No one tells you what to do; you just have to learn to do it. I learned this by experience and by reading about it before I went to college.

What things did you know about college disability services offices when you were still in high school?

Kelly: My high school counselor told me to talk to the Disability Resource Center, as did the students guiding the tour when I asked questions and they didn't know the answers. So, making frequent visits and setting up meetings with the disability center helped calm my fears and made me feel like I could do this (college) easily because they were there to help with anything I needed.

Tommy: I didn't know much about them until I visited colleges and went to the disability services offices. This is something that is very different from high school, where your services are agreed upon in the IEP. It is very important to meet with disability services at any college you visit. The disability services people I met while visiting colleges explained to me what I had to do in order to get accommodations and services. The procedures for obtaining services were similar at various colleges, but sometimes the services themselves were different. I am very confident in myself to get the necessary services today because I have been doing it for 3 years now.

ENABLING COLLEGE PROFILE

University name: University of California, Berkeley
University website: http://www.berkeley.edu

One of America's best-known universities, Berkeley is also famous for being the place where activist students with disabilities in the 1960s organized to demand services for themselves. They were successful, and to this day, Berkeley's Residence Program serves freshmen and transfer students with physical disabilities who have never directed their own personal care. Over two semesters (one academic year), students learn the skills to coordinate their own medical and personal care needs (University of California, Berkeley, 2007). The Residence Program has accessible rooms reserved in the Berkeley residence halls.

Berkeley also has a wheelchair rescue and repair service and a transportation program that picks up students who become stranded within city limits. Other services include scholarships, tutoring, career counseling, on-campus van/tram service, and accessible public transportation.

Berkeley's TRIO/Student Support Services Project works to promote retention and graduation at the university. TRIO programs are federal outreach programs that support the needs of students with disabilities. The Berkeley program provides support services to students who are new to Berkeley, students at risk academically, students with challenging disabilities, and students who are preparing for graduate school or careers. Some of the many services include assistance in transitioning from high school or community college, disability management counseling, and assistive technology assessment and instruction.

Berkeley is regularly ranked among the best schools in the nation and is, consequently, very selective in admissions. The college has approximately 23,000 students.

CHAPTER 2 RESOURCES

This chart compares the characteristics of students with disabilities who are likely to succeed in college and those who may not yet be ready to succeed.

What Makes a Successful College Student?

Student Characteristics	Successful	Unsuccessful
Commitment	<ul><li>Wants a college degree</li><li>Sets goals</li><li>Sticks to plans</li><li>Is self-disciplined</li><li>Jumps on assignments</li></ul>	<ul><li>Is in college to please others</li><li>Lacks real goals</li><li>Vacillates</li><li>Lacks discipline</li><li>Spends too much time on social activities</li></ul>
Skills	<ul><li>Has college prep background</li><li>Is well-organized</li><li>Is computer literate</li></ul>	<ul><li>Took few challenging high school classes</li><li>Has messy work habits</li><li>Rarely uses computer</li></ul>
Advocacy	<ul><li>Uses assistive technology</li><li>Believes in self</li><li>Is self-aware</li><li>Understands own disability</li><li>Can describe necessary accommodations</li></ul>	<ul><li>Fears or ignores assistive technology</li><li>Has learned helplessness</li><li>Has unrealistic expectations</li><li>Denies own disability</li><li>Does not ask for accommodations</li></ul>
Independence	<ul><li>Has a plan to handle personal care at college</li><li>Knows money and time management</li></ul>	<ul><li>Expects college to provide personal care</li><li>Is disorganized regarding finances and schedule</li></ul>

The laws governing high school and college are very different. This chart compares the roles of students and institutions at both stages of the education process.

Legal Principles Governing U.S. Students With Disabilities

High School	College
Laws: IDEA (Individuals with Disabilities Education Act) and Section 504 of the Rehabilitation Act	Laws: Section 504 and ADA (Americans with Disabilities Act)
Children with disabilities are entitled to a free appropriate public education.	Colleges are only required to make the academic adjustments necessary to be sure they don't discriminate against students with disabilities.
Accommodations and services are usually designed to maximize a student's potential.	Accommodations are granted to level the playing field.
School districts are responsible for identifying children with disabilities and providing special education supports and services.	Colleges may not seek out students with disabilities; students must identify themselves as disabled and provide documentation to obtain accommodations.
School districts must provide rehabilitation counseling, medical services, personal aides, and other services needed.	College provides physical, academic, and program access. Services of a personal nature are the responsibility of the individual student or family.
Parents are the primary advocates for their children's accommodations and have access to all records and grades.	Students are responsible for advocacy and obtaining accommodations. Students are considered adults and must give permission in order for parents to view records and grades.
Individualized education is aimed at the child's special needs.	Programs need only be made accessible.

WEBSITES RELATED TO CHAPTER 2

DISABILITY FRIENDLY COLLEGES

http://www.disabilityfriendlycolleges.com
An online resource with charts detailing colleges and universities that go beyond ADA in services for students with physical disabilities. This site also contains transition information, many articles, links, and a blog.

U.S. DEPARTMENT OF EDUCATION

http://www.ed.gov
This site contains information on the rights and responsibilities of students with disabilities.

U.S. DEPARTMENT OF JUSTICE

http://www.usdoj.gov
Information can be found here on disability rights and the significant federal laws impacting the education of students with disabilities such as ADA, Section 504, and IDEA.

WRIGHTSLAW

http://www.wrightslaw.com
This site contains information about special education law, education law, and advocacy for students with disabilities.

THE COLLEGE
SEARCH

HOW would you answer if your guidance counselor were to ask you today for the top three criteria by which you plan to choose a college? Location? Curriculum? Cost?

Kelly, one of the students interviewed at the end of this chapter, said she had known ever since she was a child that she wanted to attend the University of Kentucky. "My destiny was UK," she said simply. Kelly has congenital muscular dystrophy and needed a variety of accommodations and personal care assistance, something no longer offered at UK. However, this school and its journalism program were what she wanted, so she took time to make repeated visits to the campus with her mother to assess potential accessibility issues and to get to know the disability services staff.

Many people are not as certain as Kelly about what they want in a college. If you are not yet ready with your criteria, now is the time to sit down and think through each item that you will be considering and its significance for college choice. Although it is clearly important to assess the expertise that each college's disability services department possesses in working with your type of disability, there are at least a half dozen other considerations of equal or greater importance.

TYPE OF COLLEGE

Your first consideration should be whether you wish to attend a 4-year college or a 2-year college. Four-year colleges and universities offer the opportunity to earn a bachelor of arts (BA) or bachelor of science (BS) degree. These institutions may be public or private. The variety of studies is extremely wide in this type of school, and one can major in areas ranging from music to business to physics. The spectrum of cost and selectivity is equally wide across America's universities. Private schools are usually more expensive than public ones, and of course, the more highly ranked the college itself, the more selective it can be in choosing its students.

Two-year colleges may be community colleges, technical colleges, or even private junior colleges. These schools offer either associate of arts (AA) or associate of science (AS) degrees. Some students who attend a 2-year college begin a career upon graduation with their associate's degree. Others elect to transfer to a 4-year college to complete a bachelor's degree. Associate's degrees may be obtained in technical fields, such as computer sciences and electronics technology, or academic fields, such as business administration, nursing, and liberal arts.

Two-year colleges are considered a good option for students with physical disabilities because they offer the opportunity to become accustomed to college-level academics while still residing at home, where personal care services and other types of assistance are available.

If you take the 2-year college route with the goal of transferring to a 4-year college, remember to keep your eye on that goal. Tell your advisor about your plans, and make sure that the courses you are taking are transferrable to the 4-year college of your choice.

In recent years, the Internet has made distance learning an option for students who wish to attend at least some classes online. Even many traditional colleges and technical schools today also offer online classes and hybrid ones combining distance learning with time spent on campus.

COLLEGE CHOICE CRITERIA

After deciding between 4-year and 2-year colleges, set up a list of what you want most in a college. The listing below should help you get started, and at the end of the chapter is a College Preference Checklist.

You can copy this checklist and take it with you on college tours to track how each college meets your criteria.

Good sources of information on potential colleges include your guidance office at school, special education teachers familiar with your disability, college fairs, friends with a similar disability who are already in college, and the many college guides found in libraries, bookstores, and online. Our website, http://www.disabilityfriendlycolleges.com, specifically addresses colleges and college issues for students with physical disabilities. Once you have identified some potential colleges, you can go to their websites and search for such things as majors, class size, and disability services.

Some students today also use independent consultants called "college coaches" or "college counselors." If you are looking at selective private colleges or if your high school guidance staff is overworked, this may be useful. However, be sure to look for a coach who has had experience as a guidance or admissions counselor and preferably has worked with students with disabilities.

The importance of individual criteria for choosing a college will vary from student to student, but taken as a whole, consideration of the following factors will put you in touch with your own preferences and form the basis of your college selection.

LOCATION

The geographic location of a college may be an important factor for several reasons. Ask yourself the following questions to determine if location will be critical to your decision:

- ▶ Do I need family and other current support systems nearby?
- ▶ Do I need to be close to current medical providers?
- ▶ Can I be sure of service for my wheelchair or other equipment away from home?
- ▶ Can our college budget support the cost of on-campus housing?
- ▶ How will I commute to a local college?
- ▶ How will I transport my chair or other equipment to a college away from home?
- ▶ Do I prefer an urban, suburban, or rural college?

If you will need support from family or medical and service providers, then explore the local college options. If you have a strong desire to test your independence and live away from home, put particular emphasis on the support services of the colleges and locales that interest you. If you think you prefer to take independence one step at a time or wish to save money, consider a 2-year college followed by a transfer to the 4-year institution of your choice.

Career Goals

Why are you going to college? Do you have a career path in mind? Do you love a particular subject and want to study it in depth? Whatever the long-term reason for attending college, it will be a critical factor in determining where you go.

Discuss these concepts with your guidance counselor and begin to plan the type of education you want. Career goals will also be part of the transition planning process. If in doubt about your direction, talk with your VR counselor about aptitude testing that will indicate your career strengths and preferences.

Remember that you are not locked into any major you choose to pursue or any career path that is taking you in the wrong direction. However, having a goal ahead of you and a plan that you and your advisors can follow will help keep you focused during your college years.

Selectivity

If you have done well in high school and are considering a top-ranked university, make sure you know its requirements for grades and SAT/ACT scores. Make sure, too, that its disability services match its academic reputation. If not, you could end up with much more on your plate than a challenging curriculum. To boost your chances with highly selective schools, maximize your participation in extracurricular and community programs and hone your essay skills for the admissions process.

Cost

For many students today, cost is not just one factor—it is the only factor. Several children in college or a reduction in parental income may mean your family must look for scholarships, loans, and grants to support your college education. Discuss these issues with the financial aid offices of colleges that interest you. Public colleges are generally less expensive than private ones, and commuting is less expensive than living on campus.

The Financing College section of this chapter discusses in detail the many financing options open specifically to students with physical disabilities.

College Size/Class Size

Colleges vary greatly in size. Large, public institutions may have classes as large as 200 to 300 students. Even classes at smaller schools may be larger than you were used to in high school. Evaluate how significant this will be to your ability to learn and find your place in a class.

Large classes present physical access issues as well. Where is the disabled seating in a class of 300? Will you feel part of the class? If you use a wheelchair or scooter, can you sit with friends, or only at the far end of a row of seating? Can you hear and see the lecturer? Are laboratory stations accessible? Is the distance between your classes overwhelming for travel with a wheelchair, scooter, or walker?

Conversely, large campuses are more likely to have an accessible bus or shuttle system with wheelchair lifts. Be sure to check on these things with disability services and other students when visiting campus.

Public Versus Private Colleges

If cost is the prime consideration, the answer may be a public college or university in your home state, where tuition is lowest. Other factors, including smaller student/professor ratios or the desire to attend a college affiliated with your faith, may lead you to a private school. Pay particular attention to the level of expertise in the disability services departments of smaller, private schools, as they may have had less experience working with students with your type of disability.

Campus Life

College is more than academics, especially if it is your home away from home. Check out things that you may require or desire such as:
- a health clinic,
- veterans' services,
- adaptive sports,
- accessible transportation on and off campus,

- ► religious organizations,
- ► clubs,
- ► student government, and
- ► honor societies.

OFFICE FOR STUDENTS WITH DISABILITIES (OSD) EXPERTISE

When you have narrowed your choices to five or six colleges, begin to zero in on the expertise of the Office for Students with Disabilities (OSD). You will find the OSD page on the college website, but the name of the office will vary from college to college. Office of Special Services, Disabled Student Support Services, and Disability Resource Center are some examples. To find the office's webpage, enter "disability services" or "students with disabilities" into the website's search engine, and you should be directed to the page.

DISABILITY SERVICES TIP

Be wary of schools whose websites stress what accommodations they *do not* provide and those that speak in very legalistic terms about what they *must* provide. "The enlightened schools don't use just the ADA," said Jeffrey A. Vernooy, director, Office of Disability Services, Wright State University.

First, ask yourself what you will need from this department based upon your specific disability. What accommodations do you have in high school? Can some of them be replaced with assistive technology or computers? Will you need only the more common accommodations such as extra time on tests, note takers, or handicapped parking? Or do you also want to live in a dormitory and require personal care, wheelchair repair, and accessible transportation?

Ask the disability services office about these things and other supports on campus, such as learning centers and computer labs, where more individualized academic support may be available.

Finally, see Chapter 2 for lists of specific physical disabilities along with commonly provided accommodations and services. Compare these with the more extensive ones that are available at the enabling colleges profiled at the end of each chapter to determine how much accommodation you will require.

THE COLLEGE VISIT

"The admissions visit speaks volumes," said Larry Markle, director of disabled student development at Ball State University. Other disability services directors agree that there is no substitute for visiting a college in which you are seriously interested.

Our family learned this when our son was recruited heavily by a private college with a special dormitory for students needing 24-hour personal care. A friend was attending the college, everything sounded outstanding, and the college was only a half-day's drive from our home. College personnel called our son often to invite him to visit.

Touring the campus, however, we noticed many facilities that were in poor repair. We decided this college was not the sure thing we had hoped it would be and began to widen our search. Within a few months, the college announced it was in financial difficulty, and the students in the personal care dorm were told the building would be closing and they would have to transfer to other colleges.

If something does not feel right about the college, its facilities, or its attitude toward students with disabilities, it probably is not the right college for you. A well-planned visit is your best source for the information that can rule a college in or out. There are plenty of "virtual college tour" websites online, but it is best to use them as a starting point and make in-person visits to any colleges in which you are seriously interested.

On the visit, be certain to do more than take a campus tour. Schedule visits to all of the offices with which you will be working, including financial aid, disability services, and admissions. Prepare yourself before the visit so that you are ready to ask your questions yourself and advocate for your own needs. Be prepared to explain the accommodations you are currently receiving in high school. "Ask all the questions you need to about the things you are concerned about," said Jeffrey Vernooy of Wright State University. "If they can't talk about it with you, it's a red flag."

DISABILITY SERVICES TIP

"See the campus beyond the tour," advised Julie Walton, professor and disability specialist at East Stroudsburg University of Pennsylvania. "Spend more than a few hours traveling the grounds and buildings before you decide. Talk to the students in the student union or cafeteria; see if you can attend class in one of the large lecture halls."

Although it is always beneficial to attend college open house events, these are sometimes held on weekends when opportunities to attend classes and visit with students are less frequent. Add an extra day to the visit in order to do these things on your own.

Once on campus, here are the other important things to look for:

- ▶ Observe the number of students with physical disabilities. Does the school attract people with disabilities similar to yours?
- ▶ Are the dorm rooms large and accessible? Are there call buttons or an intercom for nighttime emergencies?
- ▶ How large is the campus? Is it accessible or hilly? Is there accessible campus transportation? Does winter weather impede wheelchairs, walkers, and other mobility tools?
- ▶ If the school provides personal care, meet the people who do this work. Do the students seem to work well with them?
- ▶ Are the basic services, such as curb cuts, elevators, and handicapped parking, adequate and enforced? If not, handicapped access may not be a priority.
- ▶ Do tour guides seem familiar with handicapped access issues or do they run ahead, leave you behind, or ignore you? This, too, is a clue to attitudes on campus.
- ▶ How do students with disabilities operate in the cafeteria? Is help provided with getting and eating food?
- ▶ Ask about academic services. Most schools do not offer services like scribes for homework and writing research notes or people to get books down from your shelves. Find out how other students with disabilities get these tasks done.
- ▶ Do your skills and interests mesh well with the curriculum and philosophy of the college?
- ▶ If you are used to playing adaptive sports like soccer, basketball, or swimming, ask whether these are available on campus or nearby.

After visiting most colleges, you will recognize that you will have to do more things for yourself than you did in high school. It will be up to you to decide how much responsibility you can handle as you adjust to the academic rigors of college and whether living on campus as a freshman is for you.

THE ADMISSIONS PROCESS

The ADA requires colleges not to discriminate on the basis of disability. Students admitted to the college, however, must be qualified to fulfill the requirements of the program. The admissions process involves providing the college with enough information for them to decide whether or not you are qualified to meet the college's requirements.

Requirements vary slightly from institution to institution, but for most colleges you will have to submit the following by January of your senior year of high school:

- ► college application (written or online);
- ► high school transcript of your performance from grades 9–12;
- ► scores on college entrance exams;
- ► recommendations from teachers, counselors, or others who can convey your most important skills, talents, and interests;
- ► essay or other writing sample (not required at some colleges); and
- ► application fee.

Some colleges also require an admissions interview (HEATH Resource Center, 2009a). Gathering the information, writing one or more essays, and filling out applications will take time. Begin talking to admissions offices, planning the process and, if necessary, getting a teacher to coach you in the essay portion in your junior year. During the first half of senior year, set aside time each week, if necessary, to work on the application package for each school to which you wish to apply. More about application essays and disability-related topics can be found in Chapter 4.

COLLEGE ENTRANCE EXAMS

The two exams most frequently used by colleges to assess applicants are the ACT and the ACT. The SAT also has a practice test called the PSAT. All of these tests are given several times per year and often in multiple locations around a city.

Students planning to take the PSAT should do so by early in their junior year, leaving the latter part of that year and the first half of senior year to take the SAT and/or ACT. These tests may be taken more than once and colleges fully expect that students will retake them to improve their scores.

The websites for the ACT (http://www.act.org) and SAT (http://www.collegeboard.com) offer many tools for practicing the tests, planning when to take them, and tracking your performance on the tests. College entrance exam prep courses are also available.

Early in this book we noted that the transition planning process should include written IEP goals that relate directly to high school coursework. Students planning to take the college entrance exam should work with their counselors to plan coursework in order to be prepared by senior year for the ACT or SAT. Appropriate college prep math and English courses are particularly important.

Exam accommodations. Students with disabilities may apply for accommodations on the ACT, PSAT, and SAT tests. This should be done well before taking the first test. According to the College Board (2010b), the review process for accommodations can take approximately 7 weeks. Use of accommodations in school or the existence of an IEP does not automatically qualify students for college entrance exam accommodations; accommodations must still be requested and documented.

Four types of accommodations are available:

- ▶ presentation: large print, reader, Braille, oral presentation;
- ▶ responding: dictation, tape recorder, large block answer sheet;
- ▶ timing: extended time, frequent breaks; and
- ▶ setting: small-group setting, private room, adaptive equipment.

Students usually apply for accommodations through their school, but can do so directly. The school's Services for Students with Disabilities (SSD) coordinator will apply for the accommodations online. Some accommodations require additional documentation (College Board, 2008). Information on everything related to accommodations is available from the College Board online at http://www.collegeboard.com/ssd/student.

After the testing service reviews the request for accommodations, it will notify you by letter of its decision. If the accommodations are approved, the letter will include an SSD number that should be included on the registration. The eligibility letter should be taken to the test. It is important to review the letter with your school prior to the test, as the accommodations may require that your school administer the test rather than one of the area test centers. Once approved for accommodations, students usually remain approved and do not need to apply again if they retest (College Board, 2010b).

FINANCING COLLEGE

These days, students must look very carefully at the way they will finance their college education, whether they have disabilities or not. The average total cost for only one year at a public college for 2009–2010 was $7,020 and at a private college was $26,273 (College Board, 2010a). Students can meet the cost of attending college with a variety of types of financial aid, some targeted specifically to students with physical disabilities.

FEDERAL STUDENT AID

The U.S. Department of Education administers billions of dollars in programs for college students each year. Your guidance counselor and college financial aid offices are the best sources of information on exactly which programs are available at the schools you choose. Some of these are:

- ▶ Pell Grants: Need-based grants to low-income undergraduate students. They do not have to be repaid.
- ▶ Stafford Loans: Also need-based, these are loans that must be repaid.
- ▶ Other federal programs are PLUS loans to parents and campus-based programs like Federal Work Study. Full information on federal student aid is available at http://www.studentaid.ed.gov.

State-Specific Scholarships

A number of states offer scholarships that are based upon academic merit and well within the reach of many students. Information on specific state programs and state agencies can be found at http://www.collegescholarships.org/scholarships/states. htm and http://wdcrobcolp01.ed.gov/Programs/EROD/org_list. cfm?category_cd=SGT#G.

General Scholarships

Scholarships are awarded based on academic achievement, area of interest, background, and other associations such as military service or ethnicity. Search online for these. Check, too, with your guidance office for scholarships offered in your area by:

- ▶ service organizations;
- ▶ labor unions;
- ▶ professional organizations;
- ▶ corporations, for children of employees; and
- ▶ places of worship, for members of their congregations.

Most college financial aid programs require completion of the FAFSA. This process is discussed in Chapter 4.

Disability Programs

The following financial assistance programs are available specifically for students with disabilities.

SSI. Supplemental Security Income (SSI) is not directly college-related, but is a program that pays monthly benefits to people with low incomes and limited assets who are 65 or older, blind, or disabled. Students 18 or older who have disabilities should be sure to apply for SSI through their local Social Security office or Vocational Rehabilitation counselor.

State vocational rehabilitation services. Consistent with their mission of helping people with disabilities prepare for, begin, and maintain employment, state Vocational Rehabilitation (VR) offices often assist with the cost of a college education. Be sure to contact VR and apply for services by the 11th grade.

Disability-specific scholarships. A number of organizations fund scholarships specifically for students with disabilities, as do many colleges.

The first places to inquire about these types of assistance are your guidance office at school and the financial aid and disability services offices at colleges that interest you. Another excellent source of disability-related scholarship information is the DO-IT website of the University of Washington: http://www.washington.edu/doit/Brochures/PDF/financial-aid.pdf.

CONCLUSION

It may seem a long way off, but the day when you enroll in your first class or spend your first night in the dorm is probably only a year or 2 from the day you pick up this book. The preparations stressed in this chapter will help make certain the college you choose is the one you want to stay with for 4 years or more.

Among the students interviewed, Kelly knew all through her early school years that she wanted to attend the University of Kentucky. But she still needed to resolve what she would study, her career preferences, how she would pay for college, how she would obtain the personal services she needed 60 miles from home, and how she would navigate with a wheelchair on a large campus.

Lindsey went from kindergarten until her junior year of high school as a nondisabled student. She found herself just on the brink of college and needing to manage her newly acquired brain injury and her post-secondary education plans.

Tommy knew he wanted to experience life away from home, studying psychology while living on campus. He knew VR would help with his college costs. But he was surprised to find that he would have to find his own personal care solutions at most colleges.

Dustin found that his interest in telecommunications and his need for a disability-friendly college came together at Ball State University in Indiana.

In addition to the tools in this chapter, the College Preference Checklist and the Enabling College Profile in the Resources section are designed to help you ask the right questions and get the answers you need before you choose a college. The former will help you to understand your own requirements of a college, and the latter offers a benchmark by which to judge colleges in your discussions with their administrative offices.

As you compile more and more information on colleges, applications, documentation guidelines, and your own preferences, be sure to create a special file in which to organize these materials for easy reference as you move on toward evaluating the schools to which you apply.

STUDENT INTERVIEWS

Describe the way in which you went about your college search.

Kelly: I always knew I wanted to go to the University of Kentucky. So it just felt right: my dream, my destiny. I knew I needed to be out on my own for the first time to really find myself and see how well I could survive on my own. I needed to feel that struggle to feel real and alive and have those experiences myself to truly know what I'm capable of.

Lindsey: The community college was 20 to 25 miles away, and they offered night classes at my high school. At this time, I was still adjusting to my life with a brain injury, so this was the best transition from high school into college.

Tommy: I mentioned earlier my senior project, "Colleges That Accommodate People With Physical Disabilities." I used this project to work on my college search. I realized I needed to take 2 years of senior year before graduating, because I needed to take my time in looking at all of the colleges that interested me. I was looking particularly for a college away from my home that was small and familiar with people with physical disabilities.

Dustin: I just chose based on who had the best education opportunity in my field.

Did you have career goals that played a big part in your ultimate college choice?

Kelly: UK has a great journalism program and not every college I visited had that, so yes, it weighed somewhat on my decision, but not heavily.

Tommy: Yes. I wanted to be a psychologist, but most of the schools I was interested in did have psychology as a major.

When you visited college disability services offices, what academic accommodations and personal services did you ask about?

Kelly: I talked a lot about accessibility across campus. I was really concerned with not being able to get to certain places: curb cuts, automatic doors, elevators, steps, navigation, everything. UK is such a big place, but it is big enough that they know exactly how to make it easier and direct students with disabilities to certain entrances and elevators. The big factor in my eyes is always having people around so that if I do run into that one door that does not have an automatic push button, I can wait a couple of seconds and look around and there are always people there. I rely a lot on strangers to help me in my day-to-day life.

Tommy: I asked about test taking and note takers, and I was particularly interested in living on campus.

Were SATs and ACTs an issue for you? How did you resolve accommodations?

Kelly: I only took the ACTs because I knew I was choosing a college in state. There definitely were some issues when I would go to the testing center locations. I often got sent to schools I was not familiar with and the test would be held upstairs with no elevator key, and the janitor was the only one with it, and he wasn't there on the Saturdays they held the test. Or the desks they had were not wheelchair-ready for someone in a chair to pull up and write comfortably. Little things like that where they had to make quick changes when I arrived because they had not anticipated anybody needing something different. It just took longer, was a bigger deal, and I had to ask for help with quick adaptations. And who wants to go through a mess and fight for this right before they take a test that determines their future? Changes definitely need to be made in that sense.

Tommy: Yes, they were an issue for me. I had accommodations such as using a calculator and extra time, and my OI teacher was allowed to read questions to me while administering the test, if I asked. She applied for the accommodations for me, and I took it at my school with her, not in a testing center.

How far from your home was the college that you chose?

Kelly: It is about 1 hour and 15 minutes from my home in Louisville—about 60 miles or so.

Lindsey: I took classes at my high school for two semesters (minutes from our house) before I went to the main community college campus. It was really great for me. This also allowed me to do my physical therapy and doctor appointments during the day. Then, after 2 years of community college, I transferred to the University of Kentucky. It was 100 miles from my hometown and parents' house.

Tommy: The first college I attended was in Edinboro, Pennsylvania, and that is about 800 miles from my home in Atlanta. I later transferred to a 2-year college in my hometown and then to Kennesaw State University, about 12 miles from my home.

Dustin: An hour.

ENABLING COLLEGE PROFILE

University name: Wright State University (Dayton, OH)
University website: http://www.wright.edu

Wright State may not be the only university in America with an underground network of tunnels between buildings, but it appears to be the only one that has put it to work providing disability access. Wright State's students with physical disabilities began using the tunnels to navigate the campus in wintertime back in the 1970s.

During that era, Wright State obtained a grant in support of students with severe disabilities and today's extensive program was born. The current disability services staff begins talking with students as early as junior high school through the program "Starting Wright," which can be accessed through their website. Incoming freshmen with disabilities are invited to a summer orientation that includes parents, said Jeff Vernooy, director of the Office of Disability Services.

At Wright State, daytime attendant care is provided by WSU students who have received training. Students with disabilities room with students who are nondisabled, and there is a personal care station on campus for students who need assistance during the day. A representative stressed that Wright State provides "an avenue" for students with disabilities without "doing everything" for them.

The school of 17,000 undergraduates offers courses on disability management, a technology center, career and vocational support services, note takers, adapted athletics, tutoring, reading and writing assistance, and meal assistance.

According to their disability services office, 80% of Wright State graduates with physical disabilities are employed in the first year after graduation.

CHAPTER 3 RESOURCES

This checklist contains the most significant criteria for students with physical disabilities when evaluating prospective colleges.

College Preference Checklist

Complete this checklist to determine your criteria for choosing a college. You can copy the list and as you contact and visit colleges, use it to evaluate how closely they meet your benchmarks.

LOCATION	COMMENTS
Commuting distance	
In-state	
Far from home	
Accessible campus	

COLLEGE TYPE	COMMENTS
Two-year	
Technical	
Four-year	
University	
Religious affiliation	
Other	

COLLEGE SIZE	COMMENTS
Small	
Medium	
Large	
Very large	

DEMOGRAPHICS	COMMENTS
Public	
Private	
Number of students	
Big city	
Suburbs	
College town	

SELECTIVITY	COMMENTS
Very selective	

Selective

Less selective

ACADEMICS	COMMENTS
Variety of majors	
My specific major	
Study abroad	
Internships	
Teacher certification	

HOUSING	COMMENTS
On-campus	
Off-campus	
Coed dorms	
Internet access	
Wheelchair accessible	
Roll-in showers	
Single room available	

Disability Services	Comments
Accessible transportation	
Van/shuttle service	
Personal care aides	
Emergency call button	
Experience with my disability	
Meal aides	
Wheelchair repair/ loaner	
Priority snow removal	
Course load flexibility	

Campus Life	Comments
Clubs	
Adaptive sports	
Health center	
Computer labs	
Religious organizations	
Other	

This is a sample of the form that you will complete when applying for accommodations at a college's disability services office.

Typical University

Disability Services Office
Student Intake Form

Name: _____ Date: _____

Student ID number: _____

Contact Information

Campus/local address: _____

Permanent/home address: _____

_____

Phone: _____ Cell: _____

E-mail: _____

Student Information

Enrollment status (freshman, sophomore, junior, senior, graduate): _____

Major: _____

High school attended: _____

Previous college, if any: _____

Disability:

Please check all disabilities that apply:

❑ Learning disability   ❑ Mobility/orthopedic impairment

❑ ADHD   ❑ Psychological/psychiatric disorder

❑ Hearing impairment   ❑ Chronic health impairment

❑ Visual impairment   ❑ Speech impairment

Briefly describe your disability and how it affects your daily life, particularly as a student.

_____

_____

_____

Describe the accommodations you have had in the past.

High school: _____

Previous college: _____

What accommodations are you requesting at this university?

_____

_____

_____

Please list any state or federal agencies with which you work (e.g., Vocational Rehabilitation, Veterans Administration).

Agency	Counselor
_____	_____
_____	_____
_____	_____
_____	_____

WEBSITES RELATED TO CHAPTER 3

ACT

http://www.actstudent.org

This site contains information on registration and preparation for the ACT along with other college planning tools. Click on "Students with disabilities" for information on accommodations.

COLLEGE BOARD EDUCATION PROFESSIONALS

http://professionals.collegeboard.com

The College Board site is geared toward education professionals advising students on how to prepare for college.

COLLEGE BOARD SERVICES FOR STUDENTS WITH DISABILITIES

http://www.collegeboard.com/ssd/student/index.html

This portion of the College Board website is dedicated to students with disabilities taking the various College Board exams. Other portions of the College Board website contain information on the tests and all phases of planning for college.

DO-IT

http://www.washington.edu/doit

The DO-IT program at the University of Washington serves to increase the success of individuals with disabilities in challenging academic programs and careers. Its website is particularly useful for information on funding college education.

STATE VOCATIONAL REHABILITATION AGENCY

http://wdcrobcolp01.ed.gov/Programs/EROD/org_list.cfm?category_ID=SVR#G

This is the U.S. Department of Education listing of contact information for all state Vocational Rehabilitation agencies.

CHAPTER FOUR

[PREPARING FOR COLLEGE LIFE]

YOU'VE done your research and now it's time to choose from among your piles of college literature and bookmarked websites and submit your college applications. Most students choose a manageable number of colleges to which to apply. Five or six is typical, including some that may be a "stretch" and at least one "safe" school that will likely admit you.

Remember that although you will make your choices based upon career goals, location, cost, and more, it is also important to choose schools whose disability services personnel are well-qualified to meet your particular needs and help you to become a successful college student.

THE COLLEGE APPLICATION

You can receive a hard copy of the application when you order admissions information directly from a college or an online application at the college's website. Many colleges also accept the Common Application, a single, standardized first-year application form for use at any member institution at https://www.commonapp.org, and the similar Universal College Application, at https://www.universalcollegeapp.com.

The college application is not difficult to complete, but it is important to make certain you have answered all questions, submitted all accompanying information, and paid the application fee. Failure to do any of these things will reflect on you, and it is your responsibility, not that of the college, to make certain you comply with all requirements.

College applications typically ask you about your background, your parents, your siblings, whether you plan to apply for financial aid, your secondary schools, honors you have received, and extracurricular activities in which you've participated.

ADDITIONAL REQUIRED INFORMATION

Besides the completed college application form, colleges will require you to submit several other things.

- ▶ **High school transcripts.** Students may not submit transcripts of their high school grades themselves, but must ask their guidance office to submit them, according to the directions in the application.
- ▶ **Scores on college entrance exams.** If the college requires SAT or ACT scores, these, too, must come directly from the testing organization.
- ▶ **Recommendations.** Teacher or counselor recommendations are often required. Additional letters of recommendation can be requested from people who know you well and can speak to your strengths. Examples are former employers, family friends, or leaders of religious and community groups in which you participate. Make sure to follow the directions of the college and use any forms they may require for the letter. Those recommending you may find it helpful if you provide them with a bit of specific written information about your academic record, memberships, or other activities.
- ▶ **Essays.** Not all colleges require an essay, but many do, especially the more selective ones. The best essays are original and enjoyable to read. Many colleges list several topics to choose from in preparing your approximately 250-word essay. Common essay topics include memorable literary characters, important life experiences, and unique things you would bring to the college. Although it is never necessary to disclose your disability when applying to college, these types of topics provide a perfect opportunity to do so *if you wish*. It is entirely appropriate to discuss your disability and how it has affected your life. This may help administrators understand your strengths and

challenges as they consider your application. It may also provide the admissions committee with a clearer picture of how your grades, test scores, and activities fit together (HEATH Resources Center, 2009a), as well as the unique perspective you can bring to the college. For high school students, the summer before senior year is a good time to research which schools will require an essay and to begin to draft yours, perhaps with help from a teacher. Do not forget to proofread your essay and have someone else look it over before it is sent.

▶ **Application fee.** Many an excellent application has gone astray due to failure to include the application fee, especially online. Make sure to click this box and submit your credit card information or, if applying by mail, include your check.

Most high school students submit their college applications during the first semester of their senior year. Pay close attention to the application deadlines you have recorded in your Application Checklist. In general, the application process should be completed by winter break (mid-December) of your senior year. Follow up online or by phone to be sure all of the colleges have received the necessary forms and fees.

CHOOSING YOUR COLLEGE

You can expect most admissions decision letters to arrive in March or April of your senior year. If you already have a favorite choice from among the colleges to which you applied and it has accepted you, your work is easy. If you are undecided about acceptances from several good choices, you have a very important decision to make.

Revisit your checklists of important criteria and notes from college visits. Consider the career goals that led you to decide on attending college and assess which schools will best help you achieve them. Will you feel comfortable going a long distance from your current support network? Do you need to revisit some campuses to be certain you feel comfortable getting around independently? Be honest with yourself about what services and accommodations you will need and which schools seem best able to provide them. Finally, as with any other difficult part of the college selection process, consult your guidance counselor and family.

If you are not accepted at any of your first-choice schools and may wish to transfer eventually, consider asking those schools' admissions offices what held you back. If it was your scores or your essay, then a year or two of accomplishing college-level work elsewhere may convince them that you are ready to attend their school.

DISABILITY SERVICES TIP

"Major in something you can do," said Cheryl Amoruso, director of the Justin Dart Jr. Center for Students with DisABILITIES at the University of Houston. "Even if the major seems okay, check the core requirements, like languages or math. Make sure you can do the degree first, then look for a school with the accommodations and accessibility that you need. Not all are the same."

APPLYING FOR FINANCIAL ASSISTANCE

FILING THE FAFSA

The first step in obtaining financial assistance for your education is to fill out the FAFSA. Most college financial aid programs require this form. It cannot be submitted before January 1 of the year for which you apply for aid, but it is important to do it as early as possible. The FAFSA can be completed online at http://www.fafsa.ed.gov or on forms found in your guidance office.

Complete and return all financial aid documents required by the financial aid offices of the colleges to which you are applying, being careful to meet their deadlines. College financial aid offices also can be of great help in explaining and helping to navigate the paperwork required to make students eligible for federal and state loans and grants as well as specific scholarships.

A few weeks after filing the FAFSA, you should receive a Student Aid Report. This document is also sent to the colleges you list on the FAFSA so that they can prepare your financial aid package.

College financial aid notifications will generally arrive during April of your senior year.

ASSISTANCE FROM VOCATIONAL REHABILITATION

It is important to file the FAFSA and explore financial aid options even if you anticipate aid from your state's Vocational Rehabilitation (VR) program. High school students with disabilities and older students who may have acquired their disabilities later in life can both benefit from the services offered by their state VR office.

The Vocational Rehabilitation programs in the United States were established as a result of the Rehabilitation Act of 1973. The Rehabilitation Act was designed to maximize the employment, independence, and economic self-sufficiency of people with disabilities (HEATH Resource Center, 1996).

As noted, students should apply for VR services, if they wish to receive them, during high school. Applicants are typically eligible for services if a counselor at VR determines that:

1. They have a disability.
2. Their disability prevents them from getting or keeping a job.
3. They require VR services to get or keep a job.

If students are eligible for services, they are assigned a counselor to help them access services and develop a career plan. Including VR in the transition services IEP will facilitate the move from high school to college to employment.

If postsecondary education is determined to be necessary to meet your employment goal, VR typically assists with the cost and may provide other services as well. VR may provide career assessments, assistive technology evaluations, independent living services, and counseling (DO-IT, 2010).

VR is funded at the state and federal levels, but each state has its own VR program. This is important because the services and levels of financial assistance may vary from state to state. As noted by the HEATH Resource Center (1996), an online clearinghouse of information on postsecondary education for individuals with disabilities,

in many instances, out-of-state postsecondary education is permitted, but financial assistance through the VR agency is limited to rates equal to that of in-state tuition and fees unless there is a unique circumstance for the selection of a particular out-of-state institution. (para. 7)

Students should be sure to ask exactly what the VR agency will fund toward their college expenses. Some states indeed pay more than others. As the HEATH Resource Center (1996) noted, "Under federal law, each individual VR agency must establish fees that are reasonable and fair. What is determined to be reasonable and fair varies" (para. 8). Part-time college attendance is usually sponsored "only if absolutely necessary and justified" (Northeast Technical Assistance Center [NETAC], 2005, para. 11).

Students should always discuss levels of funding available from VR and request a list of other services for which they may be eligible such as computers for use in college. Students commuting daily from home to campus should ask about transportation services and personal assistance, if required.

Your VR counselor will require you to apply for other available funding as well, including Pell Grants and state-specific scholarships (discussed in Chapter 3). Students eligible for such assistance generally receive VR funding only secondarily to scholarships and grants.

A final word about VR counselors. Because VR provides a crucial service to college students with disabilities, it is essential that your counselor always have your best interests at heart. If you feel this is not the case or that you are not being adequately informed, speak to the counselor's supervisor, or, if necessary, ask to change counselors until you are matched with someone who is truly knowledgeable and concerned with maximizing your access to college and VR services.

Once in college, you will have responsibilities to your VR counselor as well. You will be required to meet with the counselor regularly, reporting on your grades and progress toward your degree. If circumstances affecting your college program change or you wish to change your plan, your counselor should be informed. Continued funding or support depends upon progress toward your work goal and cooperation with your counselor. Remember that VR services, like college, are something for which students must establish eligibility, and gainful employment must be the plan's projected outcome.

You can find your state VR office in the phone book or at http://wdcrobcolp01.ed.gov/Programs/EROD/org_list.cfm?category_ID=SVR.

MANAGING DISABILITY-RELATED ISSUES

DOCUMENTING YOUR DISABILITY

The time to begin the process of documenting needed accommodations is well before arriving on campus. As noted, colleges must offer accommodations that ensure equal access to the curriculum and the physical campus. It is the responsibility of the student, however, to register with the disability services office on campus, request the accommodations, and provide the documentation upon which the college can base its decision about which modifications to provide.

Some students with physical disabilities may only require minor accommodations such as a handicapped parking permit. This may not require documentation. Others may need housing accommodations, academic accommodations such as extended time on tests or note takers, or assistive technology. The best time to start talking about accommodations with your chosen college is in the spring or summer before you arrive on campus for fall semester, according to Cheryl Amoruso, director of the Justin Dart Jr. Center for Students with DisABILITIES at the University of Houston. Some colleges encourage students to register with disability services as early as 6 months to a year before enrolling, so it is wise to check on this when visiting colleges.

In order for a college to determine whether or not a request for disability-related accommodations is appropriate, the student must provide proof of the existence of a disability, a current diagnosis, and justification for the accommodation requested. Most colleges require that documentation be provided by a qualified professional, with that person's credentials stated in the documentation. A physical disability alone may be documented by a physician, whereas an accompanying learning disability may require documentation by a licensed psychologist.

Your college disability services office will have documentation guidelines available for you, but most adhere generally to the seven essential elements listed by AHEAD. These are:

- ► the credentials of the evaluator(s);
- ► a diagnostic statement identifying the disability;
- ► a description of the diagnostic methodology used;
- ► a description of current functional limitations;

▶ a description of the expected progression or stability of the disability;

▶ a description of current and past accommodations, services, and/or medications; and

▶ recommendations for accommodations, adaptive devices, assistive services, compensatory strategies, and/or collateral support services.

Documenting your disability according to the procedures of your college disability services office is the first step in obtaining the services you have already identified as necessary to your college success.

OTHER FORMS AND DOCUMENTS

Once you have registered with disability services and submitted the required documentation, you will begin to meet with your counselor in the disability services office to discuss services and accommodations. In most colleges, after you have worked out your accommodations, you will sign an agreement stating what those accommodations and/or services are.

Forms required may vary from college to college, but in general, expect to complete the documentation of disability form, an application form, a documentation of services provided in high school, if requested, and a form granting consent to release information. Sample documents can be found in the Resources sections of Chapters 4–6. Students are expected to request accommodations at the beginning of a semester and in accordance with disability services deadlines. The disability services department does not typically handle housing accommodations, but it can usually assist you in locating the proper contact in the housing department.

MANAGING YOUR PERSONAL CARE

"Directing personal care is the biggest hurdle," says Larry Markle, director of Disabled Student Development at Ball State University. "If students talk to me in their sophomore or junior years, I let them know that their parents won't be coming to school to do that (personal care) with them. We discuss these issues first."

University disability services personnel are virtually unanimous in their agreement that the biggest obstacle to college success for students with serious physical disabilities who live on campus is unfamiliarity with obtaining and directing their personal care. Unless they choose to attend one of the handful of colleges that provide personal care services or choose to commute to school and live at home, students must arrange for their personal care themselves. Even students who commute to a local college face this issue if they need assistance eating meals, using the bathroom, or traveling to and from campus.

DISABILITY SERVICES TIP

What are the most important things students and families can work on to prepare for the college experience? "Time management, planning and organizing, self-care, independent living, medical care close to the institution, and replacement medical supplies and services," said Julie Walton, Professor, Disability Specialist, East Stroudsburg University of Pennsylvania.

As Markle noted, the time to begin planning for your personal care on campus is when you begin visiting colleges. Unless you are well-versed in hiring and directing attendants, it will be important to ask colleges about the types of assistance they provide in this area. Colleges are not required to provide personal care assistance, and their responses will run the gamut from being completely hands-off the process, to providing assistants, to providing help in hiring an attendant.

FOUR EXPERIENCES WITH ATTENDANT CARE

▶ Jenna attends a school in the Midwest that once provided personal care but no longer does. Her university's disability services office gave her the names of local agencies that provide personal care aides. Jenna had very little experience working with anyone except her family for her personal care, and she advises incoming students to recognize that once they get to college, hiring and training an aide is their responsibility.

▶ Stephanie attends a Southeastern college. Her school had never provided personal care but did take time to help her find it. The disability services office set up meetings for her with representatives from three different agencies the summer before Stephanie started school. Stephanie said they worked to ensure that she got quality care and that she was very happy with the situation.

▶ David attends a small Mid-Atlantic college. He required a personal aide but was told that only a student registered at the college could serve as an aide. David and his family were not happy with this situation, so David's father rented a house in the town where the college was located so that he could serve as David's aide himself.

▶ Matthew, also from the Southeast, was interested in a small, religiously affiliated college about 45 minutes from home. Matthew was originally offered admission, a scholarship, and a promise of a student to be his roommate and aide. The offer was later rescinded, and Matthew instead chose to attend a college that provided personal care.

These are true stories from acquaintances and our website, although names have been changed. Their message is that personal care is so essential to college success that it must be discussed early and often with colleges. You must decide whether you are ready, as Jenna and Stephanie were, to hire and direct attendants.

If so, begin by making an assessment of the activities of daily living (e.g., showering, getting out of bed, eating) with which you need help. If you only require limited help, such as in the cafeteria or library, you may be able to ask your roommate or a friend. For more extensive needs, a personal care attendant may provide better and more reliable assistance (HEATH Resource Center, 2009b). This type of attendant is usually referred to as a PCA, PC, attendant, or aide.

Personal care attendant jobs are well-suited to student schedules, especially if the student attendant is studying in one of the health care fields and is seeking experience. Request referrals for personal care attendants from the university disability services office, your Vocational Rehabilitation counselor, college placement office, home health care agencies, and other students with disabilities who employ aides. If your area is served by a Center for Independent Living (CIL), then inquire there about PC referrals and learning how to employ and train a PC. The Independent Living Research Utilization Program (ILRU) maintains a list of U.S. centers at http://www.ilru.org/html/publications/

directory/index.html. See Chapter 6 for more tips on recruiting and hiring attendants.

MEDICAL CARE

Another related and important issue is medical care. Often students with physical disabilities have several physicians as part of their support network at home and will need to provide for this care if they go away to school. According to Jacob Karnes, director of the Disability Resource Center at the University of Kentucky,

> Students with medical needs don't think about not having their own doctor at college. They need to have some kind of medical services nearby, so they should go ahead and talk to the university health service ahead of time and get to know them.

Evaluating Assistive Technology Options

Many students with physical disabilities rely heavily on assistive technology. From computers and smart phones to voice recognition systems, key guards, and trackballs, technology helps them to access and complete college coursework as well as to maintain contact with friends, professors, and service providers.

Something as simple as a cell phone or smart phone mounted on a power wheelchair can provide security and networking capabilities. In the same way, assistive technologies can help you access your coursework. To find the most appropriate technology, one should have an assistive technology evaluation. This may already have been done as part of your IEP transition plan by your school district's occupational or physical therapy department. An evaluation may also be obtained through the Vocational Rehabilitation department, if you are a client. They will assign a rehabilitation technologist to assist you in determining your technology needs and goals as a college student and to recommend both high-tech and simple solutions.

Once you have chosen a college, it is important to include the disability services office in your assistive technology planning, as it will be able to inform you about technology available for students on campus. You may wish to begin both eliminating technology that is no longer needed for class work and utilizing technology that will approximate that available at your college while in high school.

An excellent guide to assistive technology is *Computer Resources for People With Disabilities*, published by The Alliance for Technology Access (2004). The following examples of the technologies available to assist college students in minimizing the limitations accompanying various physical disabilities are described in greater detail in the above book (on pages 181–284), along with many others.

- ► Computer input aids:
  - ▶ **Alternate keyboards**. Keyboards that vary in size, layout, and complexity in providing input to a computer.
  - ▶ **Key guards**. Keyboard covers that have holes for each key and are used to avoid striking unwanted keys if fingers are unsteady.
  - ▶ **Voice recognition systems**. Also called speech recognition systems, this technology allows the user to speak to the computer rather than using a keyboard and mouse to input data.
  - ▶ **Electronic pointing devices**. These devices allow the user to control the cursor on the screen using ultrasound, an infrared beam, eye movements, nerve signals, or brain waves.
  - ▶ **Pointing and typing aids**. Usually a type of stick used to strike the keys on the keyboard, these can be held in the mouth, worn on the head, strapped to the chin, or held in the hand.
  - ▶ **Joysticks**. Another way to control the cursor on the screen with a stick that pivots, these can be plugged into the computer's mouse port.
  - ▶ **Trackballs**. A trackball, or trackball mouse, is a ball held by a socket in a docking area that also has buttons and is used in place of a mouse. The ball can be rolled with the thumb, fingers, or palm to move the cursor. The buttons control other functions.
  - ▶ **Arm and wrist supports**. Devices to stabilize and support the arms while using a computer.

► Processing Aids:
- ⊙ **Word-prediction programs**. Computer programs that allow the user to select a word from an on-screen list that is generated as the user types the first one or two letters of a word he wishes to use. Useful for typists who need to reduce the number of letters typed or type more quickly.
- ⊙ **Electronic reference tools**. Electronic dictionaries, encyclopedias, atlases, and other reference works.

► Computer Output Aids:
- ⊙ **Screen readers**. Software programs that provide verbalization or "reading aloud" of everything seen on the screen. Can also provide Braille output.

Mainstream technology is expanding quickly with products that make books accessible for people with physical disabilities, as well. College texts are often available on CD, electronic reading devices like Amazon's Kindle and Barnes & Noble's nook are becoming less expensive, and books are also available on special websites for people with difficulty accessing printed materials.

CONCLUSION

Preparation and planning are the twin themes of the successful journey to college with a physical disability, just as they are with many important life experiences. No matter how excited you might be about the prospect of a first trip to a foreign country, for example, you would not simply purchase an airline ticket and go. You would be sure you were prepared with a passport, reservations at an accessible hotel, and perhaps some language courses.

Similarly, students with physical disabilities cannot expect to simply arrive on the college campus and jump into their studies and activities. (In truth, no student can do that.) In order to succeed in the 4 or 5 years that you are there, you must do more than submit an application and be accepted. You must arrive on campus in the fall ready to access your coursework and social life through appropriate accommodations, physical assistance, and assistive technology. Just as in high school, you will need the proper support systems to do so. Unlike in high school, in college it is up to you to identify these services and begin the process to obtain them as completely as possible before arriving on campus for your first class.

STUDENT INTERVIEWS

What criteria did you use to evaluate those schools that accepted you?

Kelly: I toured just about every major college in the state: Northern Kentucky, Eastern Kentucky, Western Kentucky, and UK (University of Kentucky). Western right away was an obvious "not-going-to-work" because of the giant hill. Eastern was accessible but still needed more improvements for me to feel comfortable getting around independently. Northern was the second most accessible in my eyes, but they did not offer my major. My destiny was UK. It is the biggest college in the state, and the most accessible and accommodating in my eyes. I was risky and only applied to UK, so I was pretty much counting on getting in, and like I said, it was my destiny because here I am.

Tommy: The academics, the people at the disability services offices, and location.

Describe your relationship with your VR counselor with regard to college.

Kelly: We basically meet in the summer once a year, and I update her on my current status, send her my grades and transcript, and talk about gearing up for my career path. She offers me suggestions of what I should be doing, but has no clue of how much I can physically handle in a workload and expects too much of me, considering my condition. VR and most everyone I've met in the VR field is absolutely clueless about relating to lives of people with disabilities.

Lindsey: VR counselors have large caseloads, and students can sometimes get lost in the shuffle. The best way to guarantee that I wasn't just another name on her list was that I regularly checked in with my counselor.

Tommy: I have had several VR counselors, but the latest one that I have has been better because she is disabled like I am. However, she seems to have a very large caseload, and I think that gets in the way of her knowing me as well as I would like. I have run into a couple of policies that are not too friendly for students with physical disabilities who attend college, especially involving out-of-state college attendance and reduced course load. At the end of each semester I have to report my grades to her, and once a year we have met to discuss my case plan. VR has also provided transportation to campus.

Did VR tell you about all of the services that they could provide for college, or did you have to ask about specific ones? Which did you use?

Kelly: It's basically a "don't ask, don't tell" business. I had to ask for every single resource and was still denied most services. I had to ask for personal care assistance, help with books, and a laptop and printer because of writing difficulties. However, funding for my education was denied.

Lindsey: They paid some tuition, gave me $500 for books, bought me a laptop (a bare bones one, but it did the job), paid for my driving lessons, and [paid for] the electric scooter.

Tommy: I had to ask. After my dad had a car accident and could not drive me or help me shower, we found out we were eligible to receive transportation and personal care help, but we did not know this before the accident.

Dustin: It's hard to tell because I'm not sure if my counselor even knows what all programs they have. I know they will pay for your schooling and help with technology for you to be able to work on homework and such. So far I only use the funding for school from VR.

Was there anything special that you had to buy, do, or learn before starting college classes?

Kelly: Well, getting my "not-so-good" laptop that VR provided for me was a need that took a while, but it finally arrived a couple of weeks after starting my classes. That is the most essential thing for any college student with a disability, because you are able to use e-mail and look up information online instead of physically going out to do those things.

Tommy: I already used computers pretty well and had a technology evaluation and had my computer set up with a trackball and accessible tray. So I was pretty well set up.

ENABLING COLLEGE PROFILE

University name: University of Illinois at Urbana-Champaign
University website: http://www.uiuc.edu

At its inception in 1948, the University of Illinois at Urbana-Champaign's (UIUC) program of postsecondary education for persons with severe physical disabilities was the first such program in the U.S. Today many surveys of the completeness of disability support programs still rank this university number one.

UIUC was first with many other services. These include creation of a transitional living program for students needing assistance in the performance of activities of daily living, having accessible buses, a formal study-abroad program for students with disabilities, rehabilitation service fraternity, collegiate wheelchair basketball teams for both men and women, and varsity letter awards to athletes with disabilities.

Sixty to 80 students per year enroll in the Disability Resources and Educational Services program. Many others who do not register for the program are nonetheless attracted by the accessibility of the school and its curriculum.

UIUC services include basic wheelchair maintenance, lift buses, driver assessment and training, private rooms with semiprivate bathrooms, meal assistance, 24-hour emergency personal assistance, career counseling, scholarships, tutoring, a state-of-the-art computer lab, emergency call systems in all rooms, and housekeeping and maintenance services.

UIUC staffers confirm references, conduct background checks, and train personal care aides, but it is the students themselves who do the interviewing and hiring.

University disability service officials describe UIUC as "significantly more successful in retaining and graduating students with disabilities than the national average" (Collins, Hedrick, & Stumbo, 2007, p. 30).

Approximately 31,000 undergraduates attend UIUC.

CHAPTER 4 RESOURCES

College Application Timeline

Summer Prior to Senior Year:
- ► Create a list of all colleges in which you are interested.
- ► Visit listed colleges in your area or on vacation trips.
- ► Begin talking with college disability services offices.
- ► Discuss options with a Vocational Rehabilitation counselor.

September:
- ► Finalize the list of colleges to which you wish to apply.
- ► Send for applications or download information from websites. Create a checklist of application deadlines, fees, and other info for all colleges.

October:
- ► Make final college visits.
- ► Begin filling out applications.
- ► Register for and take the SAT or ACT.
- ► Begin drafting your application essay, if required.

November:
- ► Apply to colleges with early decision and rolling admission policies first.
- ► Request high school transcripts from your guidance office.
- ► Research financial aid opportunities.

December:
- ► Complete all college applications.
- ► Receive early decision responses.
- ► Apply for scholarships.

January:
- ► Submit FAFSA as soon after January 1 as possible.

February:
- ▶ Contact colleges/check online status to make sure applications are complete.

March/April:
- ▶ Begin to receive admissions decisions and financial aid awards.
- ▶ Make final decision and accept admission and aid.

May:
- ▶ Submit disability services documentation or schedule an appointment to meet.

June:
- ▶ Have your guidance counselor submit your final transcript to your chosen college.

This is a sample of a typical form completed by your physician verifying your disability, diagnosis, and possible accommodations.

Typical University

Disability Services Office
Verification of Disability

Student's name: _____

Date of birth: _____

I am requesting academic support services through the Disability Services Office at Typical University. I hereby authorize the health care provider listed below to release to Disability Services the information requested on this form in order to determine my eligibility for academic accommodations.

Student signature: _____ Date: _____

To be completed by a certified health care professional:

Physician's name: _____ Date: _____

Address: _____

_____

License/certification #: _____ Phone: _____ Fax: _____

Diagnosis(es): _____

_____

Level of severity: ❑ Mild ❑ Moderate ❑ Severe ❑ Remission

Duration: ❑ Permanent ❑ Chronic ❑ Temporary

Procedures/assessments used to diagnose this student's condition:

_____

_____

Treatment and/or medications currently being used:

_____

_____

Functional limitations caused by this condition and/or its treatment:

_____

_____

Identify how this condition might impact the student in an academic setting:

_____

_____

Recommended accommodations:

_____

_____

Physician signature: _____

WEBSITES RELATED TO CHAPTER 4

ALLIANCE FOR TECHNOLOGY ACCESS

http://www.ataccess.org

The mission of the ATA is to increase the use of technology by children and adults with disabilities and functional limitations. Their website offers publications, information on ATA centers, and other resources for using technology to minimize physical disabilities.

BOOKSHARE

http://www.bookshare.org

This website offers online books and periodicals for readers with print disabilities. Bookshare is free for all U.S. students with qualifying disabilities.

FREE APPLICATION FOR FEDERAL STUDENT AID

http://www.fafsa.ed.gov/index.htm

This is the official website for completing the FAFSA form online. The form is required by most college financial aid programs.

INDEPENDENT LIVING RESEARCH UTILIZATION

http://www.ilru.org

ILRU provides research, education, and consultation in the areas of independent living, the Americans with Disabilities Act, home- and community-based services, and health issues for people with disabilities. Their website features publications, training, discussion boards, and a directory of Centers for Independent Living across the U.S.

CHAPTER
FIVE

ACADEMIC SUCCESS

DEFINITIONS of academic success can be as individual as students themselves. To one college student, academic success may be graduating summa cum laude in French literature, while to another it may mean obtaining the general management knowledge to start a small business.

However you define it, academic success begins with surviving your first year at college in good standing and making it to sophomore year. At some orientation programs, a dean or college president may tell the students to look carefully at the people to their right and left, because one of the three of them will be gone before graduation.

The retention rate for colleges of average selectivity in the U.S. is usually cited as being around 50%, meaning only 50% of freshman stay through graduation. With added challenges, students with physical disabilities face steeper odds (Horn & Berktold, 1999).

No one wants to be that one student out of every three who fails to make the grade. To get through your first collegiate year successfully, you will need solid planning, good study habits, and the ability to advocate for your own accommodations.

COLLEGE COURSEWORK AND ADVISING

Selecting the appropriate coursework for your first year is an important step toward academic success. Recognizing this, colleges assign each freshman an academic advisor, typically during orientation. Your academic advisor will assist you with course selection, and it is important not to disregard the advice he gives you. This person will have seen many freshmen come through the college and will know a great deal about the courses offered and the professors who teach them. As the advisor comes to know you, he will be better able to assist you in choosing the best courses for your program.

You should make sure your advisor is aware of your reasons for attending college, what you hope to do with your college degree, and anything about your disability that impacts how you learn. If you communicate honestly with your advisor about your goals and interests, it will be easier for him to suggest courses, internships, and other opportunities. Many students have the same advisor from their major field right through graduation. At some schools, however, a student with physical disabilities may have an advisor from the disability services office. Even if your advisor does not come from disability services, it may be a good idea to consult that office about courses that you are considering. As with your Vocational Rehabilitation counselor, if for some reason you feel you have not been assigned an appropriate advisor, ask to be assigned another.

When selecting courses, it is important to be aware of courses required for graduation in your major and take them as early as possible. Leaving a large number of required classes for the last couple of semesters may make them harder to schedule. Make sure that your schedule is balanced, with some more demanding courses and some that are less demanding each semester or quarter. By reviewing the college catalog or class syllabus and talking with advisors, you should be able to determine which courses require large amounts of reading, labs, and papers; what types of tests are given and their frequency; and the style of teaching the instructor uses (DO-IT, 2008). Students can even consult "professor rating" websites with names like pickaprof.com or ratemyprofessors.com to see how previous students have rated individual professors at their school.

Course Load

In addition to the types of courses selected for your schedule, consider the number of courses you can handle successfully and how this is impacted by your disability. Having a physical disability or chronic illness can mean that it takes you longer to prepare assignments. Learning disabilities, too, may impact your course load. For example, if you can successfully manage three courses per semester, but not the usual minimum of four, you may want to consider applying for a reduced course load. This is probably most important as you begin college, because the academic demands will be greater than they were in high school, and you will require time to adjust. It is possible that, with one or two semesters under your belt, you will find yourself ready for a heavier course load.

Course load can affect more mundane issues such as financial aid, insurance, and eligibility to participate in sports or live in residence halls. To be considered a full-time student for these purposes, you may have to maintain a certain course load (usually 12 credits). Failure to do so may mean ineligibility for financial aid, Vocational Rehabilitation services, and coverage under your parents' auto or health insurance. If you are considering less than full-time status, then it is important to check on these issues first.

LEARNING STYLE

Your learning style, too, has a bearing on the types of courses you will take, as does the set of study skills you bring with you to college. Learning style refers to the way you learn best. Do you prefer to see visual presentations, hear or read the material, or perhaps have actual hands-on experience with the material, as in a lab? Everyone learns differently and combines several of these elements.

By the time you begin your freshman year, you should be able to identify any academic skill areas that you need to strengthen. Some colleges require students to take placement tests to determine how equipped the student is for enrollment in their college courses. Failure to reach the minimum scores will mean the student must take additional learning support courses in areas such as reading, writing/grammar, and mathematics/algebra.

Even if you have no need for remedial work, you may want to use the services of the learning centers, tutoring centers, or student success offices found on most campuses. These offer such services as assistance with specific course work, counseling, and first-year advising. Many campuses also offer free study skills courses, and some college departments offer study groups and assistance in their particular discipline.

"UNIVERSITY 101"

Most incoming freshmen are required to take a course variously named University 101, Freshman Seminar, or a similar title indicating an introduction to college in general and your particular university as well. It may sound like an easy class that students are tempted to skip once in a while, but in reality these courses teach the ins and outs of success on the college campus. Students learn everything from the rules of the university to skills such as time management and note taking. Students leave the course understanding more about their own reasons for being in college, their learning style, and their role in the campus community, and they learn to avoid many of the pitfalls that lead to failure in those incoming freshmen who do not graduate. Remember that you are responsible for both your successes and failures in college, and blow off this course at your own risk!

OBTAINING ACCOMMODATIONS FOR COURSEWORK

Each semester (or quarter, depending on the type of academic calendar) students must request the accommodations for which they have been approved. The process for obtaining accommodations is discussed in Chapter 4, and types of disabilities and possible accommodations are listed in Chapter 2. See Figure 1 for a breakdown of responsibilities in requesting and providing accommodations.

In your first semester, advising and scheduling may have been completed during orientation. However, for the rest of your semesters, you will begin the process well in advance. Let's say that your approved accommodations include note takers, test-taking accommodations, and priority registration. You will want to make your requests of the disability services office in plenty of time to obtain them without delay. You may need to submit a "request for early registration" form, or make a special appointment with the disability services office to complete registration. Be sure to let them know if you will need advising or assistance with registration.

In some colleges, the disability services office prepares letters to your instructors outlining your accommodations. They will give them to you to deliver as you begin your classes. These letters explain that you

Responsibility for Accommodations

Student:

- Self-identifies with disability services as having a disability as early as possible prior to beginning classes.
- Provides documentation of disability if directed by disability services.
- Meets with disability services to determine appropriate academic accommodations.
- Obtains letters of notification for professors from disability services, if required.
- Speaks individually with each professor about accommodations for each course.
- Informs the disability services office if academic accommodations are not appropriate or if a problem or disagreement with a professor arises.

Faculty:

- Works with student and disability services to implement the appropriate accommodations for the course.
- Can request assistance or clarification from disability services regarding accommodations.

Disability Services Office:

- Conducts intake interview with student. Explains accommodations, policies, and procedures.
- Receives documentation from student and is responsible for keeping it confidential.
- Determines whether the student qualifies for academic accommodations.
- Recommends appropriate accommodations.
- Provides letters, assistance, and clarification for faculty if necessary.
- Requests updated documentation from student when necessary.
- Provides support to student in the event of difficulties with accommodations.

Figure 1. Responsibilities of various parties in providing student accommodations.

have a documented disability and state the accommodations for which you are eligible and how to arrange for them. The letter may also offer the professor assistance from the disability services office in working with you. Procedures may differ from college to college, but generally it is expected that the student with accommodations will contact her professors personally, deliver the letter if applicable, and discuss the accommodations. This may be done after the first class meeting, or the student can e-mail the instructor and request a meeting.

DISABILITY SERVICES TIP

"The best time to talk to disability services about accommodations is in the summer—some even do it in the spring before they come here," said Cheryl Amoruso, director of the Justin Dart Jr. Center for Students with DisABILITIES at the University of Houston. "Don't wait to get book lists for books on CD from professors until the second week of class. Plan ahead. We get the books on CD from publishers 80–90% of the time."

In the case of the accommodations mentioned above, the student will have registered early and explained her accommodations to all professors during the first week of class. A note taker will have been requested from among the students in the class, and copy paper may have been provided by the disability services office for that purpose. Testing will likely occur at the same time as the rest of the class but in a location where the student can receive any necessary assistance (e.g., with writing answers or manipulating a calculator). This is usually the disability services office. It is up to the student to schedule all test taking as soon as the dates are known.

Other types of accommodations for which students with physical disabilities may be approved include special equipment, laboratory assistance, and textbooks in alternate formats. If reading from a CD on your computer works better than manipulating heavy textbooks, you can work with the disability services office well before the class begins to order the books on CD when available.

COMMUNICATING WITH INSTRUCTORS

It is important to stress that when you meet with your instructor you are requesting that he or she agree to the accommodations that have been approved for you. It is not appropriate to make demands or to be angry, even if the instructor is not as cooperative as she might be. If the instructor does have questions, reservations, or disagreements with accommodations, you must take this up immediately with disability services personnel. It is their responsibility to resolve any disagreements over recommended accommodations.

GRIEVANCE PROCEDURES

Most professors understand the protections afforded to students with disabilities and will be cooperative in helping you to achieve maximum access to their classes. If the disability services office is unable to obtain the accommodations to which you believe you are entitled, you can file a complaint with the U.S. Department of Education Office for Civil Rights. Information and complaint forms are available at http://www2.ed.gov/about/offices/list/ocr/complaintprocess.html. By law, complaints of discrimination must ordinarily be filed within 180 days of the last act of discrimination.

LEARNING DISABILITIES

It is not unusual for some forms of physical disability to be accompanied by a learning disability. It is also not uncommon for students to begin attending college unaware that they have a learning disability and find that they are having considerable difficulty with the curriculum. In either case, when a learning disability, as well as a physical one, is diagnosed as being present, the process for obtaining accommodations may be a bit different for the learning disability.

Learning disabilities are not visible and you are not required to disclose them. However, if you know that you have a learning disability and you want to request services or accommodations from the disability services office, you must self-identify and request the accommodations. The documentation requirements may include recent neuropsychological testing and evaluation as well as a specific diagnosis.

Once this documentation is approved, you will work with the disability services office to plan accommodations in much the same way as you would for a physical disability. Accommodations for learning disabilities may include priority registration, alternative format textbooks, extended time on examinations, peer mentoring, counseling, and academic planning assistance.

Because college is fundamentally more academically challenging and rigorous than high school, students who find it difficult to keep up often drop out. If you suspect that you may have a learning disability, consult a qualified professional or your disability services office. A learning disability affects the way that students take in, retain, and express information. It may affect such areas as listening, written expression, reading comprehension, mathematical calculations, and many other things. Understanding the way a disability affects how they learn has helped many students obtain the appropriate accommodations. These accommodations can make the college learning process both fruitful and enjoyable for them and reduce stress and frustration.

SUCCESSFUL STUDY HABITS

Most disability services directors say that students with physical disabilities usually come to college well-prepared academically. However, the added academic challenges presented by the coursework, the new personal responsibilities, and the increased freedom can each lead to destructive study behaviors. Parents and teachers will no longer be making decisions for you. The responsibility for academic success rests with you, so make sure the following keys to success are established in your behavior from day one in college.

ORDER BOOKS EARLY

Once you have registered, you should be able to order your textbooks from the bookstore a week or two before classes begin. You may even be able to do so online. Check with the bookstore about procedures.

The benefit of ordering the books early is that you can begin reading before classes begin and get a head start on what will undoubtedly be a larger amount of reading than you experienced in high school. Another good suggestion is to do the reading for one of your fall semester courses over the summer, after purchasing the textbook. This will give you an enormous jump on your fall reading as well as familiarize you with the topic.

As mentioned earlier, you may also be able to get the books on CD through disability services. Be sure to check the syllabus for first-week assignments, as professors may skip certain chapters and not necessarily start at the beginning of the book.

ATTEND EVERY CLASS

In college, the professors rarely take attendance or keep track of student absences. They expect that you will attend class, and actually doing so is up to you. This new independence from parents and paraprofessionals may tempt you to skip one or more classes because no one will say anything about it. Don't do it. You will miss all of the material covered in class that day and undoubtedly pay the penalty when testing time comes. Miss several college-level classes and the odds are that you will not pass the course at all. Do not schedule classes during times when you know you will have to do other activities, and if you must miss a class, get the notes as soon as possible.

REVIEW THE SYLLABUS IMMEDIATELY

Beginning college students might ignore the course syllabus that instructors distribute in the first days of class. That is because they do not realize that everything they need to know about the course for the entire semester is included in that document. It will include such things as class meeting dates, topics to be covered, textbooks used, papers or other assignments to be completed, test dates and formats, and contact information for the professor.

Reading the syllabus will give you a big picture of the course and what is expected of you. It will also give you a chance to think about how your recommended accommodations will work for the course and any questions you might want to ask the professor. Familiarity with the syllabus for each course will allow you to plan your work and to include all due dates and exam dates in your planning calendar.

PREPARE A BINDER FOR EACH CLASS

Even if you are not using a notebook to take your own notes, you will want a notebook in which to keep all of the notes you obtain from your note taker, the syllabus, and other handouts. Be certain to keep the notebook organized. As the University of Washington DO-IT (2008) website for students with disabilities points out, "If your notebook is sloppy and disorganized, visualize your grades in the same vein" (para. 8).

STAY ON TOP OF YOUR READING ASSIGNMENTS

We already mentioned getting a head start on assigned reading, but don't forget to be prepared for current classes. If you take notes or highlight sections as you go along, you can return to them prior to class or exams to review the information. It is important to stay on top of the reading for all classes because the workload is greater in college. Once you fall behind, it is not only hard to catch up, but hard to follow the class lectures as well.

AVOID PROCRASTINATION

Professors won't often remind you to complete or turn in assignments. You will be expected to have read assignments before class and to turn in assignments according to dates on the syllabus. That does not mean that if a paper is due December 5 that you should wait until December 1 to begin it, however.

Try to determine how much time it will take you to complete assignments and readings and start them accordingly. This will become easier as you become accustomed to college-level work. Always utilize your planner to organize your work as soon as you receive assignments or the syllabus. Set aside a certain time each day to study and stick to it.

If you recognize that you are prone to procrastination, you can use simple strategies to make it easier to begin assignments. For example, instead of reading an entire 30-page chapter, break it down into two or three sittings. When beginning a term paper, tell yourself that you will work in steps, first brainstorming ideas, then preparing a strong outline, and finally beginning the research and the writing. Studying with a friend can help keep you on track, too, especially if you promise each other to complete specific parts of the assignment by a certain date.

DISABILITY SERVICES TIP

Students with physical disabilities who go from living at home, perhaps without a lift van, to living on a campus where they have the independence to do what they want run the risk of going overboard, said Jeffrey A. Vernooy, director, Office of Disability Services, Wright State University. "Students find there are more people to talk you out of doing work at college."

COMMUNICATE WITH INSTRUCTORS AND DISABILITY SERVICES

College students are considered responsible for their own success, but that does not mean that support systems are not available when needed. If you are having difficulty or falling behind in a course, make an appointment to talk with your instructor. Even small matters, such as questions about an assignment, should be settled right away rather than being allowed to snowball into a poorly done or missed piece of work.

Support is available from disability services as well. Personnel from that office can help with unresolved problems with courses as well as other issues such as time management and difficulty adjusting to college life.

The important thing to remember is to communicate when you are having difficulty. Chances are that whatever is getting in your way as a student, instructors and counselors have helped other students through it before.

Use Online Systems Carefully

More and more colleges today use Internet-based learning systems (with names such as Angel, Blackboard, and Course Compass) to handle tasks such as making course materials available, allowing students to turn in assignments, holding group discussions, returning student work, and posting grades, all online. Many colleges also offer courses entirely or partially delivered online.

These tools and courses can present potential pitfalls for college freshmen, but they do have some decided benefits for students with physical disabilities. A computer is an absolute necessity for a student with physical disabilities. Students should become experienced in high school in using tools such as Internet browsers and e-mail, Microsoft Word, PowerPoint, and Excel in order to prepare for college Internet-based learning and research. They should also refrain from taking any hybrid or completely online courses until they are sure enough of their learning and time-management skills to do so successfully.

That said, mature students with physical disabilities or speaking impairments can benefit from the instant accessibility of interfacing with the instructor online and taking occasional courses or coursework from their own home or dorm.

Learn Time-Management Skills

A typical college semester may include two 15–20 page term papers, 2–3 hours of reading for each hour spent in the classroom, lab assignments, study groups, and a few exams. No one will remind you of these tasks once they are assigned.

A student with a physical disability may also have to schedule special exam accommodations several times per semester and meet with disability services staff. Most students also belong to clubs and organizations, have medical appointments, and need to keep appointments with professors and advisors.

How can you keep abreast of all that goes on in a busy freshman's life? It does not matter what type of planner you use, but *it is essential* that you utilize some type of planning system from day one.

If you used a student planner in high school, you are ahead of the game. If you did not use a planner or you relied on a paraprofessional to write down the assignments and due dates for you, you must now devise a method of doing this yourself.

You will need a long-range planner that covers the entire academic year. Paper calendar-type planners are available at college bookstores and office supply stores. If your disability inhibits writing or you are simply more technologically inclined, you will probably want to use planning software on your computer or smartphone. Then do the following:

- ▶ Review the syllabus for each class and enter due dates, exam dates, labs, and reading assignments.
- ▶ Enter reminders to request needed services for each item (e.g., testing accommodations prior to test dates) from disability services.
- ▶ Enter other obligations such as appointments and club meetings as soon as they are scheduled.
- ▶ Finally, break down large reading and writing assignments into manageable parts as soon as they are assigned. Look at the length and difficulty of the assignment and determine how much time you will need to complete it. Break it down into manageable chunks and actually schedule them in the planner for specific days. For example, schedule research paper assignments such as library work, reading, outlining, and creating a rough draft exactly as you plan to complete them (DO-IT, 2008). The planner will direct you to complete the component parts a little bit each week. When you have several months before a research paper or an exam comes due, the planner can spell the difference between cruising easily to the end of the semester and late nights spent writing and cramming.

If you are not a very disciplined student or are used to working with a family member or paraprofessional, then you can use your planner to organize your daily work as well, scheduling the times of day when you will study. Certain disabilities may cause your energy or enthusiasm to vary throughout the day, so plan to study when you are at your best.

You can also include social planning and housekeeping issues in the planner. Note football games you want to attend, birthdays of family and friends, and meetings with your VR counselor.

CONCLUSION

After a semester or two, college academics and planning will become second nature, but freshmen have many adjustments to make and obligations to meet. When this is added to the special circumstances created by attending college with one or more physical disabilities, there is little room for error.

Most high school students with disabilities are used to relying on paraprofessionals and other educators during school hours and parents or siblings at home. Those who succeed in their freshman year at college do so by relying as much as possible on their own planning ability, study habits, and advocacy skills with limited assistance from friends and disability services staff.

Just as they placed their career goals and academic preparations on paper in the high school IEP process, college freshmen with physical disabilities should be prepared to think through their interests and needs, organize their work, and self-advocate when necessary in order to be successful.

For college students with physical disabilities arriving for freshman year, documenting and obtaining appropriate academic accommodations was step one. Securing additional necessary services and supports is the next step in preparing for a successful freshman year.

STUDENT INTERVIEWS

What characteristics of the college experience came as most of a surprise to you?

Kelly: Definitely the workload, even though I expected it. Also the every-day struggles that you don't realize or expect to face. Having your parents or siblings there in your house for you 24/7 to being in a dorm room by yourself needing help is hard to swallow. Although I wanted the independence, it is a drastic shock to not constantly have someone there.

Dustin: The professors really don't care whether or not you show up.

Describe any academic accommodations you had in college and how you went about obtaining them.

Kelly: I went to the Disability Resource Center for everything. I needed electronic notes from the lectures; separate testing accommodations with the use of a different location, extra time, and use of a laptop; extended time on major projects or papers; and special consideration in extreme weather circumstances, all stated in a letter that I would give to my professors within the first week of classes. I also verbally communicated what accommodations I would need.

Tommy: Right now I have a note taker, but I have to tell the instructor that I need one. I also have to tell disability services when my tests are. I look at the syllabus for each course and tell disability services when my tests are going to be. They put it in the computer, and I come in on the test day and they're ready for me. I also try to sit in front of the class, and I have priority registration, about 2 weeks before other students. I usually have no difficulty getting the accommodations I need from professors, except for once when a professor said he thought I could not do the course because of my disability. I talked to the disability services director and she straightened it out with the professor. I took the course and ended up with an A.

What experiences have you had with online or distance learning?

Lindsey: I'm a very visual learner, so while I did okay in these classes, I found the online classes very challenging. I was a regular in my instructors' offices. It was better for me that I had face-to-face instruction.

Tommy: I like it better for me because I don't have to depend on other people to help me do my work. I can do it all online and submit it myself.

How helpful was the disability services office? What services did they provide?

Kelly: They've been amazing. They will back you up 150%. They are there for you; all you have to do is ask. They can't help you solve the problems unless you address them and tell them the situation.

Lindsey: I was very close with the staff of the UK Disability Resource Center. For me, they provided services such as getting classes moved from inaccessible buildings to ones I could access, installing a handicapped push button as a sounding board when I had a problem, and getting me UK sports tickets. They also just provided general support.

Tommy: I would say that all of the schools that I attended do a pretty good job. Of course Edinboro also has van transportation and personal services.

Did there come a particular point when it dawned on you that you had to become the primary advocate for yourself in college?

Kelly: The first day of classes when I said goodbye to my mom, and truly was left on my own, to live on my own for the first time. I knew that I had to account for myself and also rely on strangers to help me be independent and do the things I can't do myself (get out of bed, shower, toileting). In a way, now that I've learned, it's a toss-up and hard to choose between what I love, being at home and having someone there for me 24/7, or having that freedom, being alone and struggling sometimes, and having some help throughout the day. It's hard to choose. If only there was a middle ground instead of the two extremes.

Tommy: Yes, it dawned on me when my parents called to ask me why I was not going to class. Then I thought that I had to start going to class and start taking responsibility for myself.

Dustin: No. I always have been the one to advocate for myself.

Describe any mistakes you made in beginning college that you would warn students to avoid.

Kelly: I learned that it's okay to struggle. It's okay to be afraid. It's exciting and exhilarating. My best advice is that you have to really want this. You have to have passion in your heart that you are willing to be on your own and frustrated when you can't do something yourself. If you don't 110% want it in your heart to be on your own for the first time, then don't go away to college.

Talk to people. Talk to your professors, people in your class, your dorm, everybody. Don't be afraid to make those connections. Being able to recognize you can't do everything yourself is a big thing.

Tommy: Go to class—even if you think you may get away with skipping a class. There is too much to learn in each class for you to miss one unless you can't help it.

Dustin: Don't get caught up in the social aspect of college too much. Have fun, but stay focused.

ENABLING COLLEGE PROFILE

University name: Edinboro University of Pennsylvania
University website: http://www.edinboro.edu

Located in a small, picturesque college town near Lake Erie, Edinboro University of Pennsylvania offers extensive support services for students with serious physical disabilities.

A unit of the University of Pennsylvania, Edinboro began by offering services to visually impaired students many years ago. Over time, Edinboro expanded its services to include many other disabilities and medical conditions.

The university provides personal care services in the dormitories themselves but also offers living skills training complete with a model apartment. Students have private rooms with a call system and aides on call 24 hours a day. A fleet of lift vans takes wheelchair users to class on time and also to destinations off campus, a plus in inclement weather. All of these services must be scheduled by the student, however.

Other services include the living skills center with an occupational therapist and rehab nurse, a wheelchair repair shop, a physical therapy facility, a recreation center, a computer lab with state-of-the art adaptive technology, meal aides, academic aides, and varsity and intramural sports.

Edinboro has more than 8,700 graduate and undergraduate students, according to its website. The site said that, for the 2009–2010 school year, 455 were students with disabilities. Of these, 83 were wheelchair users, 25 were ambulatory but physically disabled, 46 had a medical disability, and 12 had a traumatic brain injury.

Located in western Pennsylvania in the snowbelt near Lake Erie, Edinboro is noted for extreme winter weather and receives approximately 85 inches of snow a year.

CHAPTER 5 RESOURCES

STUDY TIPS FOR COLLEGE STUDENTS WITH PHYSICAL DISABILITIES

- ▶ Be aware of fatigue issues associated with your disability and plan your class and study schedules around them.
- ▶ Frequent breaks and a comfortable, quiet environment can also help prevent fatigue.
- ▶ If you need homework assistance, such as help with writing, ask your VR counselor if it will pay for a student that you hire to help.
- ▶ Use a cell phone or smartphone with an alarm to remind you of classes and study times.
- ▶ If highlighting is difficult for you when reading textbooks, use your computer or the notes function on your smartphone or other planning/communication device.
- ▶ Make sure you're using every technology you can to help you access your coursework yourself. Work with VR, disability services, and other agencies to explore such things as trackballs and voice recognition software. It's always easier when you don't have to depend upon others.
- ▶ Don't procrastinate. Recognize that completing assignments may take you longer than it takes nondisabled students and let your experience with this guide you.
- ▶ If your college has a learning center, take advantage of it when you find yourself struggling with coursework.
- ▶ Ask for help. College is expected to be more challenging than high school. That's why they make help available. Talk to your counselor, disability services, or professors as soon as you spot trouble.
- ▶ Finally, play to your strengths. Yes, you have a disability, but you have many more abilities. Focus on your strengths and build from there.

This is a sample of the form you will complete to request testing accommodations.

Typical University

Disability Services Office
Test Accomodation Request Form

Student Information

Name: _____

Student ID: _____

Phone: _____

E-Mail: _____

Course Title: _____

Department: _____

Course Number: _____

Professor/Test Information

Name: _____

E-Mail: _____

Phone: _____

Test Date: Year _____ Month _____ Day _____

Start Time: _____ a.m./p.m.

Accommodations Requested

❑ Extended time   ❑ Assistive technology

❑ Scribe   ❑ Computer

❑ Reader   ❑ Private room

Accommodation Letter

❑ By checking here, I confirm that I have provided this faculty member with my Disability Services letter authorizing my accommodations.

This is a sample of the form you will complete to request a note taker for class notes.

Typical University

Disability Services Office
Note Taker Request Form

Student's Name: _____ Date:_____

Semester: _____ Student ID:_____

E-Mail:_____Phone:_____

Note takers are requested for the following courses:

Course Number	Course Name	Professor	Class Time	Days	Location

- Please submit note taker request forms at least one week prior to first day of class.
- Students must be registered with Disability Services to receive note taker services.
- Please notify Disability Services if the above schedule changes.
- Receipt of note taker services does not excuse students from regular attendance and participation in classes.

Student Signature:_____ Date:_____

This is a sample of the form you will complete to request textbooks in an alternate format.

Typical University

Disability Services Office
Alternate Format Textbook Request Form

Contact Information

Student Name: _____

Student ID: _____

Phone: _____

E-Mail: _____

Course

Course Title: _____

Course Number: _____

Section: _____

Professor: _____

Book

Title: _____

Author(s): _____

ISBN Number: _____

Publisher: _____

Publication Date: _____

Edition: _____

Requested Format

    ❑ Electronic   ❑ MP3

    ❑ MS Word   ❑ Braille

    ❑ Audio   ❑ Large Print

Note: Please submit requests as early as possible in order to have your material in time for your first class. Submit the materials you are requesting along with this form. Submit a separate form for each book request.

Student Signature:_____ Date:_____

WEBSITES RELATED TO CHAPTER 5

ACCOMMODATIONS

http://www.heath.gwu.edu/modules/accommodations
This module on the HEATH website explains the services and accommodations offered by colleges and universities and educates students on how to obtain them.

COLLEGE SURVIVAL SKILLS

http://www.washington.edu/doit/Brochures/Academics/survival.html
This DO-IT online brochure offers tips for students with disabilities to increase their success in college.

COMMUNICATING WITH INSTRUCTORS

http://www.ncsu.edu/dso/general/communicating_with_instructors.pdf
This is a step-by-step guide to communicating with instructors about one's disability.

[PERSONAL ISSUES AND SERVICES]

THE nonacademic support services you request in college depend upon your college living arrangements as well as your disability. These services should be selected to ensure that you are able to participate in the full range of college activities.

For example, if you have decided to live on campus and cannot perform your own personal care, you will need to arrange for it. You may also need to request housing accommodations. If you are living at a college quite far from home, you must consider medical care in your new location. If you will be commuting from home to college, you may deal with issues such as daily transportation to campus or meal arrangements.

LIVING ON CAMPUS

Whether you choose one of the few schools that offer personal care services or one of the many that do not, living on campus can provide easy access to classes and plenty of social interaction. However, students with physical disabilities who choose to live on campus have special personal and organizational needs that must be met before they can succeed in their academics.

Students should discuss their personal accommodation needs with the disability services office as soon as they identify themselves as disabled. However, it is important to remember that most colleges will not provide personal care services and that issues related to housing are the province of the housing (often called residence life) department.

One of the important reasons for making campus visits during the process of choosing a college is to determine how readily they will be able to meet your housing needs. By the summer before moving to campus, you should be working with the housing department to request any necessary room accommodations for freshman year, for example a single room, a special desk, or a wheelchair-accessible room.

For the purposes of this book, nonacademic support services for students with physical disabilities are broken into "need-to-have" (meaning the student cannot function without them) and "nice-to-have" (meaning they enhance the student's quality of life, but are optional in terms of college success).

As discussed, colleges are required to make their academic programs and facilities accessible to students with physical disabilities, but are not required to provide personal services. This chapter describes how these personal services are obtained when attending a school that complies strictly with the Americans with Disabilities Act or goes beyond it to some degree ("ADA/ADA-Plus") and then at a full-service institution or "one-stop shop" that offers things such as extensive housing accommodations, personal care, and specialized transportation. In the listing of "America's Most Disability-Friendly Colleges" at the end of this book, you will find the colleges listed as either "full service" or "ADA Plus."

NEED-TO-HAVE SERVICES AT ADA/ ADA-PLUS COLLEGES

HOUSING ACCOMMODATIONS

Most college websites say that they offer housing accommodations or accessible housing. Most do not define either the types of accommodations or what they mean by accessible, however, and these things do vary greatly from college to college. Wheelchair-accessible dorm rooms may be available, for example, but the number and nature of these rooms vary considerably from school to school.

A student who has not made detailed inquiries about the housing accommodations offered in the dormitories has little recourse if he applies for an accommodation and finds it is not offered.

Information on housing should be included on the college's website, information packets, and at orientation. It is essential, however, to apply for housing as soon as you have chosen your college. Colleges do not always have dormitory space equal to the number of students wishing to reside on campus. First come, first served is often the rule. Colleges are not required to guarantee rooms to students with physical disabilities.

Get your application in early. Make sure the disability services and housing offices are aware that you want to live on campus and talk with both about any assistance they can give you. Again, while little personal assistance is required of colleges, some go well out of their way to help students, while others do not.

Conduct a review of any accommodations you may have at home, such as a raised desk, special bed, and bathroom features and make sure you have covered on your housing application every similar accommodation you will need in college.

Obtaining Personal Care Services

There is a wide spectrum of physical disabilities, so personal care assistance may or may not be something that you require. If you have had assistance with activities of daily living at home (e.g., getting out of bed, showering, dressing, toileting, eating), you should begin by making a "needs assessment" of just what you will require when living at college. Make a list of activities of daily living and be honest about how much help you need with each (HEATH Resource Center, 2009b). For example, is assistance with eating essential or do you rely on family members at home because it is more convenient?

Most colleges do not get involved in any way in the hiring and management of personal care assistants (PCAs), but some disability services offices do have contacts with personal care agencies or lists of college students looking for jobs as PCAs. Always start with that office first. Upperclassmen with physical disabilities who are already using PCAs are good sources of potential aides. If your college offers majors in the health care field, these students may also be seeking practical experience.

Even some full-service colleges use college students as PCAs because the work fits well with the college schedule and, of course, they are already on campus. Check with the college employment office.

Most areas of the country, particularly large cities, are served by Independent Living Centers (ILCs), as noted in Chapter 4. The services of specific centers vary, but their mission is to encourage and facilitate independent living for people with disabilities. Check with your local ILC; they should have either PCA referrals or training in how to find and manage PCAs.

Finally, try advertising. Many people with physical disabilities say that advertising for and hiring your own assistants offers a better chance of establishing a long-term and reliable personal care relationship than does working with an agency. Advertising for a PCA involves a bit more up-front work and commitment than going through an agency, so you may want to get a friend to help. You must place newspaper, Internet, and campus ads, but this also provides invaluable training in providing personal care for yourself over the long term.

Hiring and Managing PCAs

Several books, including *The Personal Care Attendant Guide* by Katie Rodriguez Banister (2007) and *Avoiding Attendants from HELL* by June Price (2002), discuss in detail how to find and hire personal care attendants as well as the legal responsibilities of an employer. This book is dedicated to facilitating the entire college experience for people with physical disabilities, but there are a few points related to hiring and managing PCAs in a dormitory or college apartment that will be stressed below. All are based upon student interviews, personal experience, and the above guidebooks.

Hiring PCAs

▸ Place ads in college newspapers; with departments such as nursing, physical therapy, and vocational rehabilitation; or in "blast" e-mails to people who may be able to suggest potential PCAs.

▸ Include the name of the position, a brief description of duties, and a phone number, but no address.

▸ Screen applicants by phone prior to scheduling interviews with top candidates.

- ▶ Meet candidates in a public place, not your dorm room or home.
- ▶ Ask about and contact previous employers.
- ▶ Consider a written contract including your responsibilities as well as those of the PCA.
- ▶ Keep a list of emergency PCAs from among former aides, people you did not hire, family, and friends.

Managing PCAs

- ▶ Use the needs assessment you made earlier as a training list for your PCA.
- ▶ Talk to your RA (Resident Advisor) to make sure your PCA will be given adequate access to the dormitory and dining hall, if necessary.
- ▶ Give the PCA lots of feedback, both on things that need improvement and jobs well done.
- ▶ When problems arise, try to brainstorm solutions together.
- ▶ If it becomes necessary to terminate the PCA, be calm and try to begin on a positive note. Use your emergency list if a quick replacement is necessary.
- ▶ Remember that it is ultimately up to you to improve or change a situation that does not meet your needs. You must advocate for yourself (HEATH Resource Center, 2009b).

TRANSPORTATION

Transportation is an issue for students with physical disabilities in two ways. First, those who commute to campus and cannot drive need a reliable way of getting there each day. Second, if you live on a large campus or commute to one, you will need to either plan your classes to be located close together or make sure to choose a college with some sort of accessible transportation system.

Commuting to ADA/ADA-Plus Colleges. Public school systems were required to provide accessible school bus transportation for you from grades K–12. Now, however, you must provide your own transportation. In a large city this may be as easy as using the public transit system. More likely, you will rely on family, a friend, or a nonemergency transportation company.

The latter option may be subsidized by your Vocational Rehabilitation department. Organizing this transportation to meet your class schedule and making sure you have ample time on campus to handle other matters is good practice for living independently.

Transportation on an ADA/ADA-Plus College Campus. Just as with housing accommodations, transportation is something that must be addressed when visiting potential colleges.

Most large colleges have campus-wide mass transit, and many have special shuttles or scheduled-ride paratransit. Note that especially with the scheduled ride systems, it is up to you to make arrangements for being picked up on a regular basis. Be sure to communicate with the campus transportation department well before moving to campus to find out how this works.

EATING

If you need assistance with getting food in the cafeteria, opening your lunch, or eating, it is important to have a plan to handle this at a college that does not provide personal services.

For commuters, you will primarily be dealing with one meal a day and may be able to ask a friend for assistance. One of the students interviewed for this book started by asking for assistance from people he did not know and in the process began to make some new friends.

If you need meal assistance as a resident student, it is important to check first with disability services and upperclassmen who receive help. They may be able to direct you to local agencies or students willing to work as your aide. Vocational Rehabilitation may also work with you and local agencies to provide you with assistance. The important thing to remember here is that if meal assistance will be required, check early with those involved in providing it so that you can have your services in place when classes start.

NEED-TO-HAVE SERVICES AT FULL-SERVICE COLLEGES

The schools that provide extensive housing, personal care, and transportation services are well aware of the special needs of students with physical disabilities. However, at these colleges the student is still obliged to request and manage these services. They are usually available on a fee-for-service basis.

Most schools that provide extensive disability services beyond what the ADA requires have been doing so since well before the Americans with Disabilities Act. Although their philosophies may differ, in general their approaches recognize that students with severe disabilities often are not prepared to advocate for and manage their own disability-related services upon graduating from high school and therefore do not complete college.

In the 2007 document *Using Comprehensive Postsecondary Transitional Support Services to Enhance the Health, Independence, and Employment Success of Persons With Severe Physical and/or Psychiatric Disabilities: The University of Illinois Approach*, authors Collins, Hedrick, and Stumbo discussed the importance of these services to college success.

> Fortunately, in many cases, students who need such services have developed effective skills and strategies to manage these needs on their own. However, for many others with the most severe physical disabilities this is not the case. The latter students are all-too-frequently not prepared at the time of high school graduation to effectively recruit, interview, hire and fire, train, schedule, pay, and evaluate individuals to assist them in the performance of such activities of daily living as transferring in and out of bed to a wheelchair, bathing, using the toilet, dressing, and eating, independent of familial assistance. As a result, college-based transitional support services are essential to ensure that these functional requirements continue to be effectively met while the students are away at college. In addition, educational services are needed to aid students in acquiring the knowledge, skills, and experiences necessary for them to assume responsibility for the independent management of these needs prior to graduation. (p. 2)

Housing Accommodations

At a full-service college, you will most likely have more interaction with disability services related to your housing needs, but you will still work primarily with the housing department and, once living in the dormitory, with the Resident Assistant on your floor.

In your first interview with the disability services office during your campus visit, you will receive information on the available accommodations such as single dorm rooms, hospital beds, call buttons, door openers, and nursing services. Some schools even permit the use of specialized furniture (e.g., beds, desks) from home in the dormitory. You will also learn how to request these accommodations on your housing application.

Obtaining Personal Care Services

At the colleges with personal care services, these supports are usually obtained through the disability services office or a specific program established to teach the skills of independent living. As with all other accommodations, the student must apply for such services.

In the history of disability services, the original efforts to provide personal care in a college setting are regarded as having been based on the "medical model" of institutional student care rather than on the more inclusive social model of integration of the student into dormitories with nondisabled peers. Today, the various schools take different approaches to providing the needed supports and independent living training.

For example, one university may house students with physical disabilities in a separate dorm or floor of a dorm, with on-site PCAs. Another may house them with nondisabled roommates integrated into an ordinary dorm. Still others may include the PCA and independent living under the rubric of an entire program set up to support academic success while simultaneously teaching the skills necessary to manage one's disability.

That being the case, the degree of freshman involvement with selecting, hiring, and training PCAs differs depending upon the college chosen. PCA services assist with such activities of daily living as transferring from a bed to a wheelchair, showering, toileting, catheterization, administering medications, eating, and dressing. At all of the full-service colleges, the ultimate goal is to graduate students who not only have earned a degree, but also have learned to manage their disabilities.

DISABILITY SERVICES TIP

"You need more time than you think to get ready in the morning, get around campus, and do your class work. Remember, emergencies happen all the time. Just this week, one of my students got stuck in the dorm because both elevators were shut down. Have a plan in an emergency: who to call, who to report the situation to, that kind of thing," said Julie Walton, professor and disability specialist, East Stroudsburg University of Pennsylvania.

TRANSPORTATION

Shuttle buses and even van fleets are available to transport students with physical disabilities at some full-service universities. Other, more urban universities rely more heavily on public transportation. Disability services offices should be contacted for more information on options; contact the transportation department to schedule rides.

EATING

Colleges that provide personal services are much more likely to provide you with assistance in the dining hall than those that do not. However, it is important to discuss this in your first interview with the disability services department in order to determine whether there is a fee involved and to set up any services you will need prior to freshman year.

NICE-TO-HAVE SERVICES AT ADA/ ADA-PLUS COLLEGES

College is more than a just a place to study; it is a place to expand your horizons, meet new people, and develop the skills and maturity you will soon use outside the classroom.

Nice-to-have services for students with disabilities are the ones that will help you explore the college world beyond the classroom and live comfortably as a person with a disability. Most colleges that meet or exceed ADA requirements do not have a great many of these services, but a surprising number have some of the following: disabled student organizations, disability management counseling, wheelchair repair and loaner shops, accessibility maps of campus, priority snow removal, disabled student cultural centers, adapted sports and physical education, special dietary requests, programs in disability studies, summer transition programs, and dining hall assistance.

Sports and Recreation

If you enjoy wheelchair basketball, power soccer, or adapted aquatics, you are on track to a healthy adult lifestyle. If you have not tried adapted sports or physical education, consider it.

The federal government's (U.S. Department of Health and Human Services, 2008) Physical Activity Guidelines for Americans said

> Overall, the evidence shows that regular physical activity provides important health benefits for people with disabilities. The benefits include improved cardiovascular and muscle fitness, improved mental health, and better ability to do tasks of daily life. Sufficient evidence now exists to recommend that adults with disabilities should get regular physical activity. (p. 42)

According to the Centers for Disease Control and Prevention's (1999) National Center for Chronic Disease Prevention and Health Promotion, people with disabilities are less likely to engage in regular, moderate physical activity than are people without disabilities, even though their need to promote their health is similar.

Although it can sometimes be difficult to find places to engage in adapted athletics, a number of colleges and universities do offer some type of adapted sports program. If yours does, check into it. If not, similar programs may be available in the surrounding community. Some examples of college-adapted athletics programs include:

▸ The University of Illinois at Urbana-Champaign has long had an extensive program of adapted sports and recreation. Adapted strength and conditioning, adapted men's and women's wheelchair basketball and coed track and field, intramurals, and adaptive aquatics are just some of the offerings. Illinois athletes have been mainstays of USA Paralympic teams as well as those of several other nations.

▸ Arizona State University offers a number of types of adaptive exercise equipment, a dry ramp at the pool, goalball, and power soccer.

- Edinboro University of Pennsylvania also offers a number of adapted sports and recreation programs including intercollegiate athletic competitions in basketball and power lifting. The Adapted Intramural and Recreational Sports fitness center is available for students with disabilities and is supervised daily. Equipment includes barbell weights, hand and leg weights, table tennis, air rifles and shooting traps, archery equipment, road racing chairs, indoor trainers, and track and field equipment. Other recreational opportunities at the fitness center include 3-on-3 wheelchair basketball, 5-on-5 wheelchair football, swimming, adapted snow skiing, and bowling.

- Ball State University is a big name in power soccer. Billing itself as the "fastest growing sport for power wheelchair users," power soccer began in France in the 1970s and is the first competitive sport designed specifically to be played by power wheelchair users. It is played on a regulation basketball court. Athletes with quadriplegia, muscular dystrophy, cerebral palsy, multiple sclerosis, and other disabilities enjoy the sport in cities across America and on several college campuses.

- The University at Buffalo in New York (part of the State University of New York system) offers Universal Yoga, based on collaboration with Matthew Sanford, a paralyzed yoga teacher and practitioner. The program is a joint effort of the University at Buffalo Disability Services, the Student Wellness Center, and the School for Public Health and Health Professions.

- Temple University has an organized program of sports, adapted recreation, and personal training, offering activities such as wheelchair basketball, tennis, and track and field. Temple University also offers adapted swimming and weight training.

SERVICES FOR STUDENT VETERANS WITH DISABILITIES

The needs of student veterans with disabilities incurred in war are obviously quite different from those of students with physical disabilities coming from high school or a 2-year college. However, at many colleges, the disability services office is heavily involved in the coordination of services for this group of students, and in some cases the services do overlap with those of traditional students.

Recent research at the University of Arizona (2010) has identified some of the characteristics and preferences of veterans returning to college after serving in the Middle East. This university received a Congressionally directed grant to "develop a research-based, replicable model for higher education that will recommend various programs, services, and strategies to create an inclusive campus environment accessible to student veterans, many of whom will have disabilities" (University of Arizona, 2010, para. 1). It is called the Disabled Veterans' Reintegration and Education Project (DVRE).

The university reported that students with military experience make up approximately 4% of undergraduate students and that they attend for-profit colleges at a rate three times that of traditional undergraduates. Some disability issues for students returned from military deployment are major depression (14%), post-traumatic stress disorder (14%), and probable traumatic brain injury (19%). Such students may be eligible for a variety of benefits, including GI Bill financial assistance and Veterans' Affairs Vocational Rehabilitation (University of Arizona, 2010).

The returning student veteran with a physical disability must learn to manage the recently acquired disability, the costs of college, possibly family issues, and the adjustment to a nonmilitary, academic way of life. The university reports concerns with issues such as college affordability, convenience, navigating the GI Bill, and inability to relate to younger students. Consequently, veteran students often choose community colleges, distance education, vocational schools, and the previously mentioned for-profit institutions as opposed to traditional 4-year colleges (University of Arizona, 2010).

DISABILITY SERVICES TIP

The new GI Bill brings a greater influx of veterans to her college, says Cheryl Amoruso, director of the Justin Dart Jr. Center for Students with DisABILITIES at the University of Houston. Her department works collaboratively with the college's veterans' services office, as is done in many schools: "We're trying to get a grant to serve more veterans. We serve 50 now, but we've just begun cracking it in the past 2 years."

Many colleges across the country are working to improve the quality of transitional services offered to veterans. Services offered at the

University of Arizona, for example, include campus accommodations, adaptive athletics, Guide to Personal Success Sports and Wellness Camp, assistive technology, fitness and nutrition consultation, an adaptive gym, and other campus offerings such as career services and financial aid. Arizona, like many colleges, has a student veterans' center and chapters of veterans' organizations on campus.

Services at other colleges include a detailed checklist for veterans on the website of Southern Illinois University. Other college websites list the following: increased levels of financial assistance through Michigan State University's Disabled Veterans Assistance Program; a Disability Resource Center serving veteran students with disabilities at California Polytechnic State University; and academic support, adaptive technology, physical support, career support, and vocational support at Wright State University.

The following resources can be helpful for student veterans with disabilities:

> ► http://www.studentveterans.org—This site includes information on transitioning to college, scholarships, financial aid, and other veterans organizations.

> ► http://www.veteransbenefitsgibill.com/2010/01/18/guide-to-military-friendly-colleges-and-universities—This site discusses colleges that offer military-friendly benefits such as distance learning, financial aid, and programs that count military experience toward a degree.

> ► http://schools.military.com/schoolfinder/search-for-schools.do—This site allows you to search its education database of more than 4,000 schools.

> ► http://www.allmilitary.com/gibill/top-ten-schools—This site has selected its top 10 military-friendly colleges based upon criteria such as financial aid, proximity to a military base, and policies friendly to service members.

> ► http://www.militaryonesource.com—This site includes information for transitioning veterans from all service branches.

> ► http://www.seamlesstransition.va.gov—This site provides information from the U.S. Department of Veterans Affairs for veterans and their families.

> ► http://www.militaryfamily.org—This site includes information on issues affecting military families, including education.

STAYING HEALTHY IN COLLEGE

Every college student leaving home for the first time experiences the temptation to test the limits of his new freedom. Sometimes that involves behaviors that drastically affect health. Too much partying or drinking, too little sleep, studying too late, living closely with others in a dormitory, and ignoring common colds and viruses caught there contribute to the poor health of many freshmen. Freshmen with physical disabilities are no different and are not immune even from the "freshman 15" pounds many students gain their first year eating in the university cafeteria.

But freshmen with physical disabilities have even more reasons than other freshmen for watching out for their health. For example, many have chronic medical conditions that require adequate rest or have dietary requirements that must be considered. Even without a chronic condition, students with physical disabilities may ignore advice on staying healthy and engage in behaviors that result in physical and emotional stress.

DISABILITY SERVICES TIP

"Students with medical needs don't think about not having their own doctor now that they're on campus. He's at home. You need to have some kind of medical services nearby. Go ahead and talk to the university health service ahead of time and get to know them," said Jacob Karnes, director of the disability resource center at the University of Kentucky.

The ways to avoid this are reasonable, and your mom has probably stressed them to you, but it won't hurt to reiterate them here.

- ▶ Get enough sleep. Your body will tell you when you are over-tired, so listen to it. Just because you are away from home does not mean you need less sleep than you did when you were living there. Lack of sleep can hurt your health—and your academic performance.
- ▶ Eat sensibly. Your body needs food to keep going with adequate energy. Don't constantly skip meals or "pig out" because you are now in control of the dinner hour. When in doubt, consult U.S. government or CDC websites about the appropriate content of a balanced diet.
- ▶ Try adaptive P.E. or other adapted recreation if available.

► Take time for social activities and clubs, but in moderation. Keep academics and fun in balance. Don't overload your schedule with social activities or isolate yourself, either.

Students with chronic conditions who will require medical follow-up at college should make arrangements to find a local physician before arriving on campus. Students who are physically disabled but otherwise healthy should monitor their own health and visit the campus health center when they have concerns about their health.

RESPONDING TO STRESS

Despite your best efforts to stay healthy, life goes on when you are away at college. Stuff happens and sometimes it is stressful. That is normal. A difficult course, a relationship that ends, or a parent who is ill and far away are all situations that can produce stress.

Students who have lived all or most of their lives with physical disabilities know about stress. But the addition of being on a campus far from home and pursuing a rigorous academic program might mean you occasionally need assistance from the campus counseling center or disability services office. Again, that's normal. Just search for "counseling" on the college website or ask the student life department for a referral. Make an appointment to discuss your situation with the people who are there to help.

STAYING SAFE ON AND AROUND CAMPUS

Staying safe, for students with physical disabilities, involves more than just the usual warnings against drugs, drinking, and connecting with undesirable characters on the Internet. If you are physically dependent upon others for assistance and care, you already know it is important to keep your wits about you at all times.

It is not common, but crime and accidents do happen, and it is important to acknowledge and be aware of those areas where you may be vulnerable.

Do not keep much money or other valuables in your dorm room, and if you must keep some, keep it hidden out of sight. If you notice that something is missing, be sure to notify the campus police and let them know who had access to your room and, perhaps, your wallet.

Know your own limits regarding drinking and partying. Students with physical disabilities have gotten into fatal situations on campuses because they thought they could take care of themselves after heavy drinking. Even moderate drinking can have a profound effect on people with orthopedic and neurological disabilities.

Use common sense and do not do things that you would not do at home such as drive a power wheelchair in heavy snow or go to unfamiliar areas of campus alone after dark.

CONCLUSION

College is preparation for adult life. You are there for the academic education, but the experiential and social education will also help to make you into an adult.

Having prepared in high school, you reach college ready to investigate new subjects, meet new people, and test your ability to handle the environment you have chosen.

None of your choices is carved in stone, and you may make changes along the way: transferring to a new college, changing your major, even taking a semester or a quarter off to think, work, or travel. Some of you may even decide that college is not for you.

But in the end, the result depends very much upon you. You are certainly not the first student with a physical disability to attend college, but you *are* the student in charge of *your own* college success, and you *can* join that growing list of highly successful college students with physical disabilities.

You made your plan. Your family and friends have supported you, but in the end the only one who can make you successful is you. So stay the course, reach out when you need help—and reach back, too, and help that incoming class to become successful college students with physical disabilities.

STUDENT INTERVIEWS

How did you decide whether or not to live on campus?

Kelly: I think it (living on campus) is the best thing anybody with a disability or wheelchair could do. The closer you are to your classes the better. The weather is a big factor every day, so being closer helps.

Lindsey: It was more of an access issue. I didn't drive, so living on campus was much more practical. Plus, I was able to participate in the social activities at my residence hall.

Tommy: I pretty much wanted to live on campus, so I looked for a school where I could do that. I did not consider a school where I would have to hire my own PCs because I didn't know how to do that.

Dustin: I wanted to test myself to figure out if I would be able to live on my own.

If you did live on campus for at least part of college, what types of accommodations or services did you need in the dorm, traveling to class, eating in the cafeteria, and so on?

Kelly: I was lucky to land in the premium suites that were newly developed. They have special handicapped rooms set up for people in wheelchairs. I have a sink I can pull under and a desk, too, that I can pull under. I have a raised commode that I share with another disabled female, a pull-in shower with a seat, and a handheld showerhead. I also had the university put in a door opener for my room, much like a garage door opener, that only I carry, because reaching the door handle and locking and unlocking my door was impossible for me to do before.

Tommy: Well, of course I needed a PC to help me with showers, getting up, dressing, going to bed, putting pajamas on, everything. And then for meals I needed meal aides, and in class I needed a scribe. I went to class in a van if it snowed, but if it was close enough, I drove my chair.

If you needed personal care aides, did your college provide them? If not, how did you go about finding an aide?

Kelly: Endless days of struggling research online and word of mouth through the disability resource center. My mom has been great at helping write to organizations asking for grants to help obtain funding for people to take care of me while I go away to college such as VR and the Center for Accessible Living in Kentucky.

Tommy: Yes, they did provide them at my first college.

Did you receive any help from your college in finding, hiring, or training an aide?

Kelly: Only in finding one, as they have nothing to do with providing assistants anymore. They were able to name a few nursing agencies that could help with caregiving.

Dustin: Just finding one.

What kind of experience had you had before college in hiring or training an aide?

Kelly: Hardly any. My mom was my sole caregiver.

Tommy: None, I never did.

Dustin: I just started using an aide, so it's a new process.

What advice would you give to a new college student in order to be prepared to provide for his personal care needs in college?

Kelly: Start looking as early as possible. Talk to disability services first to see if they have any student aides, looking for work, to help. Getting a reference from someone who is reliable through word of mouth is a lot safer than trying to sort through all the crazies that you will get through a newspaper ad. We did get some good workers through that, but it's overwhelming, outrageous, and hard to trust people at that point. Get someone you're comfortable with who has a clean background check and who you've set up several training sessions with and discussed the seriousness of their showing up with, and if they seem accountable, then you'll be set.

Tommy: If you are not ready to handle both the personal care and academics, you should start by going to college closer to home. Then, when you are mature enough, you can go away to college. I never met anyone who had learned to hire personal care aides already when I was in college.

Dustin: I would say disabled student development (disability services) will help you figure out how to get what you need, so don't be afraid to ask.

Were maturity, safety, time management, or organization issues for you in college? How did you deal with them?

Kelly: Time management wasn't too big of an issue. Being in college is a distraction in itself, so just knowing that I tire easily, I had to really stay on top of my work because I knew I couldn't stay up late and do it. Safety hasn't been too big either; I live practically downtown and do go out alone a lot, just not at night.

Tommy: Yes, they were. Not safety. I did pretty well with that. I didn't go out drinking and I got enough sleep. On maturity, time management, and organization, I didn't do very well the first time around. However, when I went to Chattahoochee Tech, and later Kennesaw State, I began to use my smartphone as an organizer and planner.

ENABLING COLLEGE PROFILE

University name: University of Houston
University website: http://www.uh.edu

It should be no surprise that the University of Houston goes beyond the letter of the ADA in its services for students with physical disabilities. Its Justin Dart Jr. Center for Students with DisABILITIES (CSD) was named for the "father of the Americans with Disabilities Act."

Justin Dart, Jr. was the son of the founder of Dart Industries and the grandson of the founder of Walgreen's drugstores. According to the University of Houston's (2008) CSD News, Dart was a self-described "super loser" in a family of "super winners" when he contracted polio at the age of 18. He had attended seven high schools without graduating from one.

By the time Dart had completed his polio treatment, his ability to walk had been limited, but his consciousness had been raised, and he became a tireless humanitarian and advocate for disability rights.

Dart attended the University of Houston from 1951–1954, earning bachelor's and master's degrees, but was denied the right to teach because of his disability (University of Houston, 2008). Instead he became a successful businessman and later a dedicated humanitarian. He headed the Federal Rehabilitation Services Administration and was awarded the Presidential Medal of Freedom in 1998.

In addition to providing what CSD Director Cheryl Amoruso describes as "typical disability services for most colleges," UH also has adapted sports, wheelchair repair, and a 24-hour attendant care program in one dormitory. The attendant care program is provided through the University Health Center.

"As much as you can, think through everything about college. What do you want to do?" said Amoruso. "Focus on your strengths. Students with disabilities are often focusing on areas of difficulty. Encourage students in their strengths and build on them."

CHAPTER 6 RESOURCES

This is a sample of a form used to request accommodations in your student housing.

Typical University

Disability Services Office
Housing Accommodation Request Form

Student Name: _____

Student ID: _____

Phone: _____

E-Mail: _____

Current Academic Status:

❑ Freshman   ❑ Sophomore   ❑ Junior   ❑ Senior   ❑ Graduate

Date of Registration With Disability Services: _____

Previous Housing Accommodations: _____

Accommodations Currently Requested: _____

Note: Housing accommodation requests must be submitted to Disability Services at least one week before the deadline for receipt of housing applications. Please see the Residence Life webpage for housing information.

To Be Completed by a Physician:

Please provide a brief description of the student's disability, including severity and issues that impact university residential living.

_____

_____

_____

Which of the following accommodations are applicable to this student's disability?

☐ Wheelchair-accessible room   ☐ Uses service animal

☐ Wheelchair-accessible toilet and sink   ☐ Strobe light

☐ Roll-in shower   ☐ Braille signage

☐ Room on first level   ☐ Other:_____

☐ Attendant access

_____

Describe the accommodations needed. _____

_____

Explain how the requested accommodations relate to the student's disability.

_____

_____

Describe any possible alternatives, should the requested accommodations not be available.

_____

_____

Physician's Signature: _____ **Date:** _____

This is a sample of an ad you might place in order to hire a personal care assistant at college.

Advertisement for a Personal Care Aide

Those experienced in advertising for personal care assistance recommend giving an honest yet positive description of the job. Stick to the basics, but be sure to mention any special requirements such as driving. If you are able to pay more than minimum wage, or perhaps an occasional bonus, saying so in your ad is a plus.

Target ads to newspaper job listings (especially the "medical" section), e-mail blasts, or colleges with nursing, physical therapy, or disability-related departments.

SAMPLE AD

Wanted: Aide for busy college student/power wheelchair user.

Personal care, some lifting required. Assistance needed twice

per day: 6:30–7:30 a.m. and 9–10 p.m. Must be dependable.

Cobb County location. Call ##########.

These sample interview questions are designed to ensure a safe and successful working relationship with the aide whom you hire.

Suggested Personal Care Aid Interview Questions

These questions were compiled from Banister (2007) and Price (2002).

- Why are you interested in this job?
- Tell me a bit about yourself.
- Have you had experience assisting people with physical disabilities?
- Is lifting/transferring a person weighing 115 pounds a problem?
- Do you have reliable transportation?
- Can you give me the names and phone numbers of two or three references I can call?
- Tell me what you understand this job to be.
- May I have your phone number?
- Do you have another job(s)?
- If so, what are your hours there?
- Can we meet for a personal interview at The Commons on campus at noon on Thursday?
- Please make sure to call if you can't make it.

WEBSITES RELATED TO CHAPTER 6

NATIONAL WHEELCHAIR BASKETBALL ASSOCIATION

http://nwba.org

Consisting of more than 200 basketball teams across 22 conferences and seven divisions, the NWBA was founded in 1948. Today it includes men's, women's, intercollegiate, and youth teams throughout the United States and Canada.

UNITED STATES POWER SOCCER ASSOCIATION

http://powersoccerusa.net

This website is for power soccer, the first competitive team sport for power wheelchair users. The site lists information on teams across the U.S. and how to get involved.

GLOSSARY OF TERMS

ACADEMIC ACCOMMODATIONS: modifications to the delivery of instruction or other academic features of a course to ensure equal access by a student with a disability, while not fundamentally altering the academic program itself.

ACT: a college entrance test measuring high school achievement and college readiness.

ACTIVITIES OF DAILY LIVING: actions that are part of an individual's daily routine such as personal hygiene, dressing, and eating meals.

ADAPTIVE SPORTS: sports modified for players with physical disabilities.

ALTERNATE-FORMAT TEXTBOOK: a college textbook offered on CD or in other medium.

AMERICANS WITH DISABILITIES ACT (ADA): since 1990, the civil rights guarantee for persons with disabilities in the United States.

ASSISTIVE TECHNOLOGY (AT): technology that is used to improve or maintain the functional capabilities of persons with disabilities.

ASSISTIVE TECHNOLOGY EVALUATION: an assessment by a rehabilitation technologist or other professional to determine what types of hardware and software may help a person with a disability improve his functional capabilities at work, home, or school.

ATTENDANT CARE: personal care provided to a person with a disability by an aide.

BLACKBOARD: also known by names such as Angel, Course Compass, and WebCT, these Internet-based systems allow professors to post course materials, grades, assignments, and other information for their students.

CHRONIC ILLNESS: a disorder that is long-lasting, recurrent, or persistent.

COLLEGE PREP CURRICULUM: coursework taken to prepare a high school student for college.

COMMON APPLICATION: a common, standardized college application for use at any member institution. The Universal College Application is used similarly.

COURSE LOAD: the number of courses taken per semester or quarter.

DISABILITY MANAGEMENT PROGRAM: a college program focused on understanding one's disability and learning to manage it as a step toward independent living.

DISABILITY SERVICES OFFICE: the department on campus that assists students with disabilities in accessing the curriculum and receiving services and accommodations needed for academic success.

DISABILITY STUDIES: an interdisciplinary academic discipline that examines disability as a social, cultural, and political phenomenon.

DISTANCE LEARNING/DISTANCE EDUCATION: delivery of course content online.

DOCUMENTATION: written confirmation, by a professional, of a student's disability.

FREE APPLICATION FOR FEDERAL STUDENT AID (FAFSA): a form required by most college financial aid offices as the first step in applying for financial assistance.

FAMILY EDUCATION RIGHTS AND PRIVACY ACT (FERPA): a federal law stating that college records cannot be disclosed to others, including parents, without the permission of the student.

HOUSING ACCOMMODATIONS: changes in the usual dormitory housing to meet the needs of a student with a disability.

HYBRID CLASSES: courses delivered partly online and partly in the classroom.

INDEPENDENT LIVING SKILLS: abilities and knowledge one must have in order to live on one's own.

INDIVIDUALS WITH DISABILITIES EDUCATION IMPROVEMENT ACT (IDEA): the law governing the K–12 public education of students with disabilities.

INDIVIDUALIZED EDUCATION PROGRAM (IEP): for public school students receiving special education services under IDEA, the IEP is a written statement for meeting the needs of each individual child with a disability. The IEP is developed, reviewed, and revised regularly in meetings.

INTAKE INTERVIEW: a student's initial interview with the disability services office.

LEARNING STYLE: the conditions under which one learns best, usually involving a combination of the senses.

MEAL AIDES: assistants who help students with physical disabilities to eat meals on campus.

NEEDS ASSESSMENT: evaluation of the specific needs of a person using personal care services.

NOTE TAKER: someone assigned to take notes for a student who is physically unable to do so.

PARAPROFESSIONAL: in K–12 public school, an employee assigned to assist a student with physical disabilities in class or with personal needs.

PARATRANSIT: a transportation system, typically involving minibuses, that is not on a fixed schedule and is equipped with wheelchair lifts or ramps.

PEER MENTOR: an older student who acts as an advisor or guide to a student transitioning to college, primarily in relation to academics.

PELL GRANT: need-based federal grant to low-income undergraduate students.

PERSONAL CARE ATTENDANT (PCA OR PC): an aide who assists someone with a disability in performing personal care activities such as dressing, showering, grooming, and toileting.

PHYSICAL DISABILITY: a physical impairment that substantially limits one or more major life activities.

PRIORITY REGISTRATION: early course registration often offered as an accommodation to students with disabilities.

REHABILITATION TECHNOLOGIST: a professional trained to evaluate the technology needs of a person with a disability and to recommend both high-tech and simple technology solutions.

RELATED SERVICES: in K–12 public school, support services such as speech pathology, audiology, physical and occupational therapy, school health services, and transportation that assist a student with a disability to benefit from special education.

SAT: a standardized college admissions test formerly known as the Scholastic Aptitude Test. The practice test for the SAT is called the PSAT.

SCRIBE: a person who writes at the dictation of a person with a disability (e.g., while taking an exam).

SECTION 504: a section of the Rehabilitation Act of 1973 that prohibits discrimination on the basis of disability by any program or activity receiving federal financial assistance. Virtually all public and most private colleges receive federal assistance.

SELF-ADVOCACY: actively seeking the help one needs to pursue one's goals; speaking up for oneself.

SELF-DETERMINATION: belief in oneself as a capable person while at the same time understanding one's strengths and limitations.

SELF-IDENTIFY: to disclose one's disability to a university.

SERVICE ANIMAL: an animal trained to perform tasks for people with disabilities.

STATE-SPECIFIC SCHOLARSHIP: a scholarship that must be used within a certain state.

STUDENT SUCCESS SERVICES: a college department (often under another, similar name) that offers support services such as counseling, advising, and help with mastering specific coursework.

Study skills courses: training in effective study habits.

Support network: people and services that one relies upon for support in daily life.

Transfer: the process in which a person in a wheelchair moves to or from a bed, chair, or toilet.

Transition planning: under the IEP process, preparing for the student's move from high school into the adult world, including college.

Transition services: under the IEP process, those services designed to assist students with disabilities in moving from the world of school to the adult world, including college, employment, and other options.

Universal design: the design of products, buildings, and many kinds of services, to be usable by the greatest number of people in the population without adaptation.

University 101: a freshman course (often with another title) that introduces the student to college in general, as well as the specific university.

Vocational Rehabilitation counselor: an advisor who works for the Vocational Rehabilitation service helping people with disabilities to obtain employment and greater independence.

Vocational Rehabilitation (VR) office: a government agency with the mission of maximizing the employment, independence, and economic self-sufficiency of people with disabilities. Each state has its own VR program.

APPENDIX

America's Most Disability-Friendly Colleges

More detailed information on specific services offered at the colleges listed below can be found on my website: http://www.disabilityfriendlycolleges.com.

FULL-SERVICE COLLEGES

These are colleges that provide such services as personal care, special transportation, independent living or disability management training, wheelchair repair, adaptive sports, and other services described in detail in the profiles at the ends of the previous chapters of this book.

- ► University of California at Berkeley
- ► Edinboro University of Pennsylvania
- ► University of Houston (Houston, TX)
- ► University of Illinois at Urbana-Champaign
- ► Wright State University (Dayton, OH)

ADA-PLUS COLLEGES

These are schools that go beyond the requirements of the Americans with Disabilities Act in providing services to students with physical disabilities. Services vary considerably among the colleges.

- ► Arizona State University (Tempe, AZ)
- ► University of Arizona (Tucson, AZ)
- ► Ball State University (Muncie, IN)
- ► Boston University (Boston, MA)

- California Polytechnic State University, San Luis Obispo
- California State University, Northridge
- University of California, Davis
- University of California, Irvine
- University of California, Los Angeles
- University of California, Santa Barbara
- University of California, Santa Cruz
- University of California, San Diego
- Cleveland State University (Cleveland, OH)
- Colorado State University (Fort Collins, CO)
- College of New Jersey (Ewing, NJ)
- University of Connecticut (Storrs, CT)
- University of Delaware (Newark, DE)
- Dowling College (Oakdale, NY)
- East Carolina University (Greenville, NC)
- Emory University (Atlanta, GA)
- Emporia State University (Emporia, KS)
- Florida State University (Tallahassee, FL)
- University of Florida (Gainesville, FL)
- University of Georgia (Athens, GA)
- Georgia Institute of Technology (Atlanta, GA)
- Hofstra University (Hempstead, NY)
- Hope College (Holland, MI)
- Humboldt State University (Arcata, CA)
- Southern Illinois University (Carbondale, IL)
- Indiana University (Bloomington, IN)
- University of Iowa (Iowa City, IA)
- University of Kansas (Lawrence, KS)
- Kent State University (Kent, OH)
- University of Kentucky (Lexington, KY)
- University of Massachusetts, Amherst
- University of Massachusetts, Dartmouth
- University of Memphis (Memphis, TN)
- Central Michigan University (Mt. Pleasant, MI)
- Michigan State University (East Lansing, MI)
- University of Michigan (Ann Arbor, MI)
- Southwest Minnesota State (Marshall, MN)
- University of Minnesota, Twin Cities

- University of Missouri, Columbia
- University of Missouri, Kansas City
- Montana State University (Bozeman, MT)
- New York University (New York, NY)
- State University of New York, Binghamton
- State University of New York, Buffalo (also called University at Buffalo)
- State University of New York, Stony Brook
- University of North Carolina, Greensboro
- North Carolina State University (Raleigh, NC)
- University of North Dakota (Grand Forks, ND)
- Northern Kentucky University (Highland Heights, KY)
- Ohio State University (Columbus, OH)
- Pennsylvania State University (University Park, PA)
- Ramapo College of New Jersey (Mahwah, NJ)
- Rutgers University (Camden, NJ)
- St. Andrew's Presbyterian College (Laurinburg, NC)
- Salisbury University (Salisbury, MD)
- San Francisco State University (San Francisco, CA)
- San Jose State University (San Jose, CA)
- Stanford University (Stanford, CA)
- Stephen F. Austin University (Nacogdoches, TX)
- Temple University (Philadelphia, PA)
- Texas A&M University (College Station, TX)
- The University of Texas at Austin
- University of Vermont (Burlington, VT)
- University of Washington (Seattle, WA)
- Wayne State University (Detroit, MI)
- University of Wisconsin, Madison
- University of Wisconsin, Stevens Point
- University of Wisconsin, Whitewater

REFERENCES

Alliance for Technology Access. (2004). *Computer resources for people with disabilities.* Alameda, CA: Hunter House.

Americans with Disabilities Act, 42 U.S.C. §§ 12102 et seq. (1990).

Association on Higher Education and Disability. (2001). *The Americans with disabilities act: The law and its impact on postsecondary education.* Washington, DC: Author.

Association on Higher Education and Disability. (2002). *College students who have chronic diseases or medical conditions.* Boston, MA: Author.

Association on Higher Education and Disability. (n.d.). *Section 504: The law & its impact on postsecondary education.* Washington, DC: Author.

Banister, K. R. (2007). *The personal care attendant guide.* New York, NY: Demos Medical Publishing.

Centers for Disease Control and Prevention. (1999). *Persons with disabilities.* Retrieved from http://www.cdc.gov/nccdphp/sgr/disab.htm

College Board. (2008). *Get it together for college.* New York, NY: Author.

College Board. (2010a). *What it costs to go to college.* Retrieved from http://www.collegeboard.com/student/pay/add-it-up/4494.html

College Board. (2010b). *Services for students with disabilities.* Retrieved from http://www.collegeboard.com/ssd/student/index.html

Collins, K., Hedrick, B., & Stumbo, N. (2007). *Using comprehensive post-secondary transitional support services to enhance the health, independence, and employment success of persons with severe physical and/or psychiatric disabilities: The University of Illinois approach.* Retrieved from http://www.disability.uiuc.edu/files/best_practices_files/textonly/index.html

DO-IT. (2008). *College survival skills: Tips for students with disabilities to increase college success.* Retrieved from http://www.washington.edu/doit/Brochures/Academics/survival.html

DO-IT. (2010). *College funding for students with disabilities.* Retrieved from http://www.washington.edu/doit/Brochures/PDF/financial-aid.pdf

HEATH Resource Center. (1996). *Vocational rehabilitation services: A consumer guide for postsecondary students.* Retrieved from http://www.landmark.edu/downloads/vocational_rehab.pdf

HEATH Resource Center. (2009a). *College application process.* Retrieved from http://www.heath.gwu.edu/modules/college-application-process

HEATH Resource Center. (2009b). *Independent living.* Retrieved from http://www.heath.gwu.edu/modules/independent-living

Horn, L., & Berktold, J. (1999). *Students with disabilities in postsecondary education: A profile of preparation, participation, and outcomes.* Retrieved from http://nces.ed.gov/pubs99/1999187.pdf

Individuals with Disabilities Education Improvement Act, Pub. Law 108-446 (December 3, 2004).

Mason, C. Y., McGahee-Kovac, M., & Johnson, L. (2004). How to help students lead their IEP meetings. *TEACHING Exceptional Children, 36*(3), 18–24.

National Center on Secondary Education and Transition. (2004). *Parenting post-secondary students with disabilities: Becoming the mentor, advocate, and guide your young adult needs.* Retrieved from http://www.ncset.org/publications/viewdesc.asp?id=208

National Council on Disability. (2008). *The Rehabilitation Act: Outcomes for transition-age youth.* Retrieved from http://www.ncd.gov/publications/2008/10282008

National Dissemination Center for Children with Disabilities. (2009). *Questions and answers about IDEA: Purposes and key definitions.*

Retrieved from http://nichcy.org/wp-content/uploads/docs/QA1.
pdf

National Dissemination Center for Children with Disabilities. (2010).
Transition planning. Retrieved from http://www.nichcy.org/
educatechildren/iep/pages/transitionplanning.aspx

Newman, L. (2005). Postsecondary education participation of youth
with disabilities. In M. Wagner, L. Newman, R. Cameto, N. Garza, &
P. Levine (Eds.), *After high school: A first look at the postschool experiences of youth with disabilities. A report from the National Longitudinal Study-2* (pp. 4-1–4-16). Menlo Park, CA: SRI International.

North Carolina State University. (1997). *Center for Universal
Design.* Retrieved from http://www.design.ncsu.edu/cud/about_
ud.udprinciplestext.htm

Northeast Technical Assistance Center. (2005). *Vocational rehabilitation.* Retrieved from http://www.netac.rit.edu/downloads/TPSHT_
Voc_Rehab.pdf

Price, J. (2002). *Avoiding attendants from HELL.* Chesterfield, MO. Science and Humanities Press.

Rothstein, L. F. (1993). *College students with disabilities: Litigation trends.*
Retrieved from http://codi.buffalo.edu/archives/colleges/.rothstein

Section 504 of the Rehabilitation Act, 29 U.S.C. Section 706 et. Seq.
(1973).

U.S. Department of Education, Office for Civil Rights. (2005). *Students
with disabilities preparing for postsecondary education: Know your
rights and responsibilities.* Retrieved from http://www2.ed.gov/
about/offices/list/ocr/transition.html

U.S. Department of Health and Human Services. (2008). *2008 physical
activity guidelines for Americans.* Retrieved from http://www.health.
gov/paguidelines/guidelines/default.aspx

U.S. Government Accountability Office. (2009). *Higher education and
disability.* Retrieved from http://www.gao.gov/new.items/d1033.pdf

University of Arizona. (2010). *Disabled veterans' reintegration and
education project.* Retrieved from http://drc.arizona.edu/about/
veterans-reintegration-education/overview

University of California, Berkeley. (2007). *History of Cal's disabled students' program and residence program.* Retrieved from http://dsp.
berkeley.edu/history.html

University of Houston. (2008). *CSD news: Justin's legacy.* Retrieved from http://www.uh.edu/csd/newsletters/2008spring.pdf

Wehmeyer, M. (2002). *Self-determination and the education of students with disabilities.* Retrieved from http://www.cec.sped.org/AM/Template.cfm?Section=Home&TEMPLATE=/CM/ContentDisplay.cfm&CONTENTID=2337

About the Author

Chris Wise Tiedemann is a freelance writer from Atlanta, GA. Her interest in disability-friendly colleges was sparked when her son, a student with a physical disability, began the college application process. The lack of available information on college services and transition issues for students with physical disabilities led her to create the popular website http://www.disabilityfriendlycolleges.com to bridge that information gap. A 35-year-veteran writer and editor, Chris has worked as a journalist, corporate communications director, and university news editor. She holds a B.A. from Marist College and an M.A. from Duke University.

Northport-East Northport Public Library

To view your patron record from a computer, click on
the Library's homepage: **www.nenpl.org**

You may:
- request an item be placed on **hold**
- renew an item that is overdue
- view titles and due dates checked **out on your card**
- view your own outstanding fines

151 Laurel Avenue
Northport, NY 11768
631-261-6930